Egyptian Mythology and Ancient Egypt

Explore the Mysterious Ancient Civilisation of Egypt, the Myths, Legends, History, Gods, Goddesses and More That Have Fascinated Mankind for Centuries

Sophia Visconti

© **Copyright 2020 - All rights reserved.**

The content contained within this book may not be reproduced, duplicated or transmitted without direct written permission from the author or the publisher.

Under no circumstances will any blame or legal responsibility be held against the publisher, or author, for any damages, reparation, or monetary loss due to the information contained within this book, either directly or indirectly.

Legal Notice:

This book is copyright protected. It is only for personal use. You cannot amend, distribute, sell, use, quote or paraphrase any part, or the content within this book, without the consent of the author or publisher.

Disclaimer Notice:

Please note the information contained within this document is for educational and entertainment purposes only. All effort has been executed to present accurate, up to date, reliable, complete information. No warranties of any kind are declared or implied. Readers acknowledge that the author is not engaged in the rendering of legal, financial, medical or professional advice. The content within this book has been derived from various sources. Please consult a licensed professional before attempting any techniques outlined in this book.

By reading this document, the reader agrees that under no circumstances is the author responsible for any losses, direct or indirect, that are incurred as a result of the use of the information contained within this document, including, but not limited to, errors, omissions, or inaccuracies.

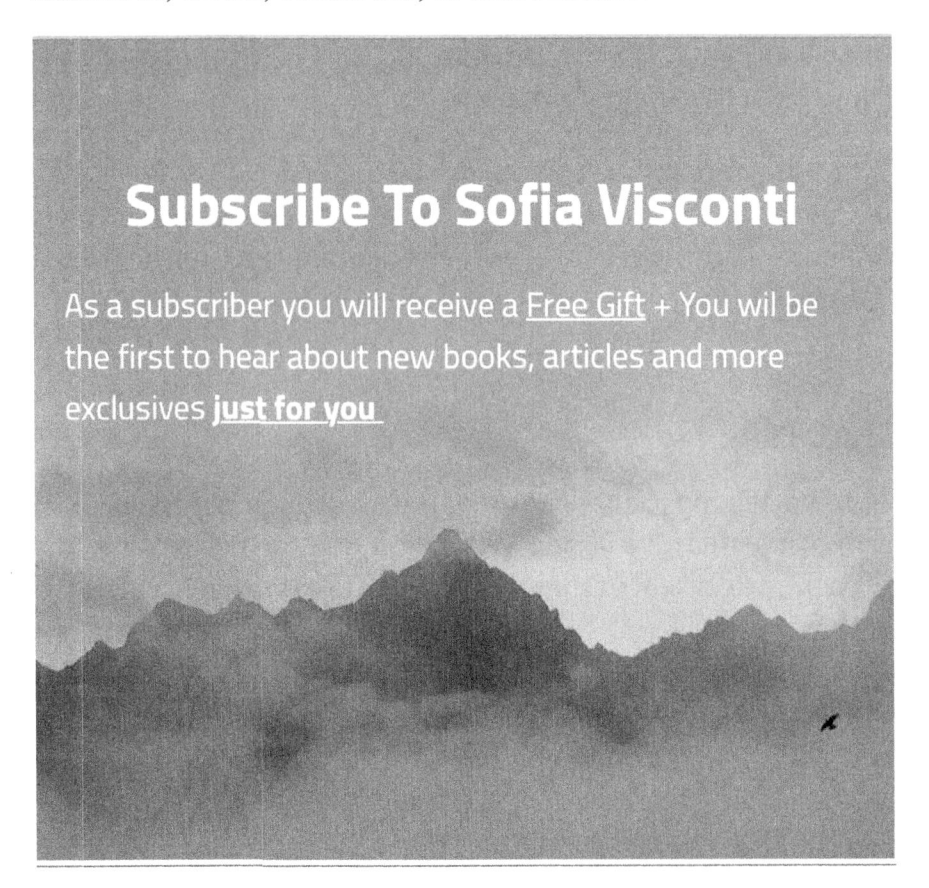

Subscribe To Sofia Visconti

As a subscriber you will receive a Free Gift + You wil be the first to hear about new books, articles and more exclusives **just for you**

Click Here

Table of Contents

Introduction

Chapter 1: Egyptian Kingdoms and Periods

    Egyptian Kingdoms

        The Formative Period

        The Classical Age

        The Empire

        The Final Phase

    Egyptian Kings

        King Djoser

        King Snerfu

        King Cheops

        King Khafra

        King Menkaure

        King Ahmos

        King Amenhotep

        Queen Hatshepsut

        King Thutmose III

        King Akhenaten

        King Tutankhamun

        King Ramses II

        Queen Cleopatra VII

Chapter 2: Egyptian Culture

    Ancient Egypt's Language

        How Did Hieroglyphic Writing "Work"?

Art, Music, and Literature in Ancient Egypt
Ancient's Egypt's Burial Rites
Science and Technology in Ancient Egypt
Interesting Facts about Egyptian Culture
- The Calendar
- Makeup and Beauty
- Cats and Pets
- Entertainment
- Cleopatra
- War and Peace
- Freedom for Women
- Beer

Chapter 3: Egyptian Pyramids & Treasures

Ancient Egyptian Pyramids: A Tale of Perfection
The Mystery of the Pyramids
The Ancient Egyptian Mummification Process
- King Tutankhamon's Mummy
- Hatshepsut's Mummy
- Ginger
- The Golden Mummies
- Nefertiti

The Ancient Egyptian Treasures and Their Fascination
Famous Ancient Egyptian Temples and Pyramids
- The Pyramids of Giza
- The Luxor Temple
- The Temple of Horus at Edfu

The Temples at Kom el-Sultan

Pyramid of Lahun

The Pyramid of Meidum

The Bent Pyramid at Dahshur

Chapter 4: Famous Egyptian Myths

Myths - A Gate to the Unknown

Genesis and the High-Level Stories of the Egyptian Mythology

The Story of Ra

Isis and Osiris

Horus and Seth

The Story of Anubis

The Book of Thoth

The Princess of Bekhten

The Prince and the Sphinx

Isis and the Seven Scorpions

Chapter 5: Egyptian Gods and Goddesses

Ra, The Sun God

   Ra-Tem

   Amun-Ra

   Ra-Horakhty

   Khepera

Shu

Tefnut

Nut

Geb

    Osiris

    Isis

    Seth

    Nephthys

    Horus

    Anubis

    Thoth

    Ma'At

    Apep/Apophis

    Bastet

    Sekhmet

    Hathor

    Ptah

    Small Deities

Chapter 6: Secrets of Ancient Egypt

    Ancient Egypt and Its Unexplained Secrets

        The Death of King Tut

        The Burial Ground of Alexander the Great

        Queen Nefertiti

        The Great Pyramid of Giza

        The Nabta Playa Stone Circle

        The Sphinx and…the Second Sphinx

        The Sphinx's Nose

    Discoveries Made in Egypt

        The Valley of the Golden Mummies

        King Tut's Tomb

    The Oxyrhynchus Papyri

    The Pyramid-Age Papyri

    Khoy's Cemetery

  The Mysterious Ancient Civilization of Egypt

    The Embalming Secrets of Ancient Egyptians

    Why They Used Astronomy to Build the Great Pyramids

    The Book of the Dead

Chapter 7: The End of the Empire

  The Beginning of the End

  Cleopatra - The Last of the Legends

  Egyptian Gods, Exist Scene to the West

Conclusion

References

Introduction

Somewhere in North Africa, on the banks of the Nile River, basking in the warm rays of sunshine of a desert climate, Egypt flourished for thousands of years. Together with it, its own gods flourished too. They cheated, they lied, they died, they came back to life, and ultimately, they faded off when new Gods and religions became the norm.

The Nile River witnessed it all: the love stories and the betrayals, the rise and fall of dynasties, the passing of the wind, and the growth of grain. Everything changed, bar from the continuous smooth flow of the river, the passing of the seasons, and the cycles of agriculture on the banks of the Nile.

Drama, death, and love flowed through the blood of the Egyptians under the watchful eyes of their gods for thousands of years.

Sometime around the year 40 C.E., a beautiful 21-year-old rolled herself out of a carpet under the amused eyes of the Emperor of Rome. Stunning (and equally cunning and erotically agile), Cleopatra was set out to win Caesar's heart.

And winning his heart is exactly what she did.

Their story ended with her suicide, his murder, and an unborn baby that had all the chances in the world to bring Egypt back to its former glory. Alas, fate had a different idea for the civilization on the banks of the Nile.

By the time Cleopatra rolled out of her famous carpet, Egyptians had already gone through more than three millennia of history. Seen as one of the world's first great civilizations, Ancient Egypt saw many changes throughout the more than 3,000 years of glory and stories.

Never before had it seen changes as abrupt, as tormenting for its natural course, and as life view-altering as they did after the conquest under the Roman Empire. Romans brought with them not only rules and legislations incompatible with the Egyptian well-being but also their gods and goddesses too. Later on, Christianity was the only religion.

The Roman ruling ended in the sixth century C.E. After more than six centuries of Roman changes, Egypt was merely the shadow of what it had once been—ready to embrace the next conquest, religion, and culture (which has survived to the date).

More than thirty dynasties preceded Cleopatra, paving her way to eternal fame. And with each dynasty, Egypt saw new technology, new gods, and new legends rising from the sand dunes and the banks of the Nile River that defined their entire growth. From the predynastic period to right before Egypt was fully won over by Romans, most of the same gods ruled over the land that depended on the Nile.

Then, everything changed—and forever so.

The glory and beauty of Ancient Egyptian mythology perfectly reflect on how those people saw life, death, war, and work. They lived under the burning suns of a desert climate, relied on the Nile River and the irrigation systems they built for food, and looked forward to an afterlife that was, perhaps, sweeter and more candid to them than the previous one had been.

Egyptians believed not only in the afterlife. Egyptians believed in personified, very human gods that got angry, made love, quarreled, and took different faces when history required it. They believed there are more than 2,000 deities ruling over every aspect of their lives: from the way the sun rises every day to how they are judged in their afterlife.

Egyptians were devoted to their religion to the point where they built massive structures to honor their gods and their beliefs. They were ready to move past their technological, human, ancient limitations to ensure that what they build and leave behind will survive for thousands of years.

Ramses II is famous for having said that he wants a pyramid to last for 3,000 years. And here we are, more than three millennia away from him, looking at the Great Pyramids of Giza in awe, unsure of how they even managed to erect such flawless, stable, and ample structures back then.

Much like the lives of pharaohs, the lives of their gods were filled with adventure, fantastic events, adultery, and even incest. They were magical lives that reflected not only on natural phenomena but on actual historical events too. Even more, the mythic stories of Ancient Egypt denote amazing interest in deeply philosophical matters: life, death, how the sun rises, and how balance is obtained from the merge between chaos and order.

We can dub Egyptians as many things, but if there is something that would be completely unfair to attribute to their culture, that is boredom. Not only did they know how to build great structures, but they also knew how to have fun. They loved beer and board games, they used makeup, and they allowed women more freedom than many other women in the ancient world lacked.

By all intents and purposes, Ancient Egypt was very much like any other modern society. Sure, they believed in different gods and were influenced by different political, economic, and social contexts. But all in all, they were very human. They were scared and happy, brave and curious, and glorious and odd at the same time. And their gods reflected all this very well.

The book at hand is meant to fuel your appetite for all the amazing (and perhaps frightening) things Ancient Egyptians were and did. From their raw history to their language and their almost obsessive focus on death and the afterlife, I plan to run you through the absolute essentials that defined 3,000 years of civilization built on the generous, fertile banks of the Nile River.

We will start with the Egyptian Kingdoms: the historical foundation everyone who wants to learn more about Egypt should know. Further on, we will explore the stories of some of the most famous Egyptian kings. We cannot fit *all* of the kings that ruled over Egypt into one book. It would probably take several books to scratch the surface of everything they did, the buildings they sponsored, and the changes they brought over their kingdom.

Our second chapter will be dedicated to the Egyptian culture and all the pillars that supported it: language, art, culture, music, science, and technology. As you might guess, all these revolved around Egyptian spirituality most of the time. However, the results spoke to millions about the passions and emotions of the people of the Nile (for thousands of years).

The third chapter will bring us a little closer to the Egyptian gods, as we will discuss the great architecture built in their names and the names of the pharaohs that represented them among mortals: pyramids and temples. Sources of vast knowledge about Ancient Egypt abound in these structures, and so is a deeper understanding of how people lived and died.

The fourth and fifth chapters of this book will discuss the very core of the subject matter at hand: Egyptian myths and gods. As you will see, they all had quite an interesting journey, and even if you are not a spiritual person, you will agree that there's a lot of truth and meaning in how Egyptians portrayed these supernatural beings.

Both the Egyptian gods and their culture are intrinsically linked to a very long list of mysteries that have fascinated the world for centuries. Therefore, we will also dedicate an entire chapter to exploring some of the most preeminent and intriguing stories and enigmas of Ancient Egypt.

Once that is done, we will proceed with the last chapter of our book: the fall of the Empire. Saddening and bitter, the fall of the Egyptian Empire is an essential part of its history and of the myths that defined the culture that continues to amaze us. Thus, it is an equally essential part to include in this book just as the fundamental myths of Egypt are, and just as the rise and fall of the different kingdoms of Egypt are.

As mentioned above, the main goal of this book is to help you gain a better, more in-depth understanding of Ancient Egyptians: who they were, who they prayed to, and how their gods helped them shape their view on life and death themselves.

My name is Sofia Visconti. I am a mythology expert who has spent her entire life reading and studying ancient civilizations, as well as the connection between their mythologies and their histories. My best selling books on Amazon and my decade-long experience in studying the ancients help me paint an accurate, comprehensive view of Ancient Egypt, its gods, and its humans.

I invite you to proceed with me on a journey of discovering not only Egyptians but also the foundations of modern culture through the eyes of what came before it. History and mythology are so tightly connected to our past and our future that it would be a major mistake to ignore them.

Yes, indeed, we might be thousands of years away from the Egyptians who embalmed their bodies for fear of turning into ghosts. But in so many ways, we are closer to ancient civilizations than we are ready to admit.

Knowing our past is bound to help us build a better future, I strongly believe the past of Egypt is one of the best lessons to teach ourselves. A culture basking in extreme sunlight and yearning for balance, Egyptians still have a lot they can show us.

Let's listen to them and their stories and come together as people of the world, ready to erect a more empathic, peaceful, and prosperous culture than everything that came before us!

Chapter 1: Egyptian Kingdoms and Periods

Of all ancient civilizations that filled history books and movie theatres around the world, Egyptians rule supreme when it comes to mystery and fascination. From the lavish colors of their papyruses to how they nailed building technology *thousands* of years before anyone else and to the legends surrounding the birth, lives, and deaths of their kings, Egyptians are an eternal source of awe.

As promised in the introduction of this book, we will talk about Egyptians from every perspective: from the very historical one (in this chapter) to the very conspiracy theory-inclined one (towards the end of the book).

The story of Egypt starts somewhere in the North East of Africa, in a land Egyptians themselves split into four divisions: Upper Egypt, Lower Egypt, the Black Land, and the Red Land. Basking in a very hot and dry climate (much like today's Egypt), this culture flourished under the Nile River's guardianship, the longest river in the world (Brier, 2001).

Upper Egypt (which, mind you, was located in the *South*) did not take much space—a mere river valley, approximately two miles in width. Lower Egypt was much larger, though, and it was located (approximately) where Cairo is today. Similarly , the Black Land was represented by the fertile banks of the Nile, while the Red Land was represented by the desert area (which was pretty much the rest of the country).

Under these conditions, it is easy to see why *all* of Egypt revolved around the Nile. From agricultural routines to religious rituals and myths, the Nile became the invisible, unspoken main character of all of Egypt.

The "gift of the Nile" (as the Greek Herodotus called it (Herodotus, n.d.)) was born in a full-blown desert but flourished for more than 3,000 years into a culture and history that are now hard to equal among all other ancient civilizations.

This is where the Egyptian civilization began. This is where its demise began as well, on the Nile River's banks, amongst the gods and the legends, between history and mystery.

Egyptian Kingdoms

Much to our pleasure, Egyptians left plenty of written accounts about their history (and where their writings might be lacking or difficult to understand; Romans and Greeks had plenty of their own accounts). Of course, all these sources tell different stories about what is virtually the same geopolitical space. But together, they can paint a fuller picture of what Egypt was, how it came to be, and how its times of ancient glory ended.

To understand Egyptian kingdoms, you should first understand that a lot of historians categorize the chronology of Egypt in four main stages (Grimal, 1992):

The Formative Period

Usually "localized" between prehistory and history, the Formative Period was a long time believed to have started together with Nile irrigations around 6,000 BCE (Roebuck, 1966).

This is the time historians understand the least, mostly due to the lack of hard evidence. However, it is quite surprising and fascinating that there *is* plenty of information for people to at least shape an idea of what that period must have been like.

Some historians place the beginning of Egypt before the great agricultural setting of Homo Sapiens. For a long time, it was believed that the jump Egyptians made from pre-historical behaviors and societies to more "modern" ways was quite sudden (and perhaps triggered by the fact that they started to embrace new technology, such as metallurgy). However, more recent evidence suggests that the journey between prehistory and what we call "ancient history" was smoother, and it took a lot of time (Grimal, 1992).

Either way, the Formative period is where the first kings are born. We are not yet talking about what historians call "The Old Kingdom", but about the "protodynastic" period that set the foundation for the next historical stage in Egypt's evolution. Three more dynasties followed their path on and off the rule of Egypt before the next historical stage was reached.

It is more than worth mentioning that the Formative Period was also when King Menes unified Upper and Lower Egypt (this happened around 3,200 BCE). This gave Ancient Egypt new wings for what is perhaps the most flourishing and exciting stage of their evolution.

The Classical Age

When people talk about "Egyptian Kingdoms," they mostly refer to the Classical Age — and the reason I am saying "mostly" is because the Old Kingdom and the Middle Kingdom are generally included in the Classical Age.

This is the stage at which Egypt started to *really* grow and flourish. If before this, Egypt was a nation (in a sense they would have defined it back then), the Classical Age completely shifted Egyptian history.

The beginning of the Classical Age is marked somewhere around 3200 BCE, and it marks the beginning of the Old Kingdom and the beginning of the Third Dynasty. Furthermore, you might also find it quite interesting to know that the Classical Age (and more specifically, the Old Kingdom) is when pyramid building was at its peak. The Great Pyramid of Giza was built for Cheops during this period, and so was the Great Sphinx.

By the end of the Old Kingdom, pharaohs and nobles started atrocious wars, and this went on for hundreds of years until Montuhotep II came to power in 2007 BCE. and finally restored order in Egypt.

Thus began the Middle Kingdom, a period in which both jewelry making and pyramid building continued to flourish until the end of this period, culminating with the Hyksos invasion. This Asian-Semitic tribe proved to be a reputable enemy, particularly because they were bringing along new technology: bronze weapons.

The Empire

As the name suggests, this is where Egypt expanded into an Empire. The New Kingdom is generally associated with the Empire stage of Ancient Egypt's historical evolution. Once the New Kingdom pharaohs evicted the Hyksos, Egypt returned to its "old ways"—but not for long.

The New Kingdom period was marked by many changes, both in terms of politics and in terms of society and religions. Egypt was reformed, and the last dynasties were seeing their demise. Despite all this, some of the greatest and most commonly known tombs belonged to this era (particularly the famous Tutankhamon's tomb, which was miraculously untouched by thieves and looters, unlike the other Ancient Egyptian tombs discovered by archeologists).

Little by little, Egypt grew from a polytheistic society to a monotheistic one. Although the New Kingdom is associated with an artistic renaissance, it is also associated with the decay of Egypt from its once shining glory.

The Ramses dynasty is largely considered to be one of the last great dynasties of Egypt. Following Ramses the Great's death, Egypt entered a period of no less than nine centuries of steady decline.

The Final Phase

This is where the story of Ancient Egypt is heading to an end. After the death of Ramses II (Ramses the Great), Egypt went through a time of political turmoil. Ramses III's heirs fought among themselves for hegemony, and, eventually, Egypt fell into the hands of Nubians, then Assyrians, then Persians, and, ultimately, Romans.

Egyptian Kings

Surprisingly enough (especially for an era when not many civilizations wrote down *their own* history), we have quite a lot of information about Egyptian kings, starting with the earliest dynasty. As it happens, much of the data is wiped up by the sands of time and change, but overall, we have a pretty good idea of what kings ruled Ancient Egypt.

One of the most important artifacts to help us on this matter are the Palermo Stone (which mentions all kings from the Third Dynasty up to the Fifth Dynasty) and the Turin Canon (a papyrus that mentions all kings up to Great Ramses) (Met Museum, n.d.)

Of course, listing *all* the kings, queens, and their achievements is too large a feat for just one chapter in one book. As mentioned before, actual Ancient Egypt history is believed to have started in approximately 3200 BCE. As you can imagine, it would be quite impossible for me (or anyone else, really) to sum up the lives, passions, fears, and deaths of so many kings in a mere chapter of *one* book. There are entire libraries out there and entire fields of study dedicated solely to following in the footsteps of every Egyptian king we know.

However, I will try to introduce you to some of the most famous Egyptian kings, as well as their most important deeds. This is important for your understanding of Egyptian history and culture and your understanding of Egyptian religion and myths (Bunson, 2002).

King Djoser

Not only is King Djoser one of the first ones to be mentioned in writing, but he is also the one to oversee the construction of the Saqqara pyramid. Although quite different from the famous pyramids we all know today, the Saqqara pyramid represented an important milestone in the evolution of the "step design."

Perhaps quite oddly enough (given the geographical separation of the two cultures), this pyramid looks eerily similar to what Aztecs and Mayans built. To date, no final explanation has been given as to how Egyptians, Aztecs, Mayans, and other culturally and geographically disparate people have managed to create buildings that are so similar in structure and appearance. But then again, as we will discuss further on, *pyramids*, in general, are still considered to be a major mystery of the ancient world.

King Snerfu

If King Djoser's pyramid is the first step pyramid to be fully acknowledged in Ancient Egypt, King Snerfu's pyramid at Dahshur is the first one to resemble what we now associate "Egyptian Pyramids" with. Also known as the "Red Pyramid," this structure is considered to be part of a trio (and it is also where King Snerfu was buried).

King Cheops

Most Westerners refer to this king as "Cheops" (after the name Greeks gave him), but for most egyptologists, he goes by "King Khufu." He was King Snerfu's son and continued into his father's legacy of building historical structures of amazing magnitude (and mystery). To be more specific, he is the reason we now have the Great Pyramid of Giza, perhaps the single most popular one in the world. This specific pyramid is so grand, so amazing, and so awe-inspiring that it has been included among the Seven Wonders of the Ancient World (and for a good reason!)

King Khafra

The apple doesn't fall far from the tree! King Khafra was King Khufu's son, and he too supervised the building of what was to become his own tomb: the second Pyramid of Giza. Furthermore, the Great Sphinx was also built in his name (and although this one might not be a pyramid, it is an equally impressive structure that has remained remarkably intact (especially given it's "only" approximately 4.5 millennia-old). Like the pyramids, The Great Sphinx of Giza is also surrounded by mystery (which we will discuss towards the end of this book, actually).

King Menkaure

Like his predecessors, King Menkaure wanted to leave his own mark on history (and, potentially, immortality). He is known to be the one who supervised the building of the third pyramid of Giza—where he also buried his only daughter in a golden coffin. Sadly, her grave was robbed (as it happened with most of the Egyptian kings' burial sites, actually).

King Ahmos

Although King Ahmos is known for buildings he started at Memphis; this is not necessarily his most important achievement. King Ahmos is largely considered to have been the first of the New Kingdom and the one who fought the Hyksos most efficiently to start the reunification of Egypt after a period of turmoil and separation.

King Amenhotep

King Amenhotep is known for his buildings and his military campaigns (much of which funded his buildings, actually). He was so revered (read: "worshipped") among the builders at Deir el-Medina (where the workmen who built the Valley of the Kings lived) that he was considered their patron for *centuries* after his death. Now, that's some legacy!

Queen Hatshepsut

Judging by how famous Cleopatra was, you'd think Egyptians had nothing against women ruling their reign. But instances of women becoming pharaohs war few and far between. Of *all* the rulers of Egypt, only six were females (Worrall, 2018). Queen Hatshepsut was one of them.

After the death of her husband (Thutmose II), her stepson (by Thutmose II's secondary wife) was left to rule Egypt. However, since he was only two years old, she assumed the role of the pharaoh, claiming that Amon-Ra had visited her mother during her pregnancy (and thus, establishing herself as a fully-entitled pharaoh of Egypt).

King Thutmose III

Queen Hatshepsut's stepson eventually came to rule Egypt (and he did so for no less than 40 years!). He is considered to have been a military genius (sometimes likened to Napoleon Bonaparte himself). One of his greatest feats was conquering most of Palestine. His reign, however, also dishonored Queen Hathsehput's name and monuments.

King Akhenaten

Although he was named Ahmenothep IV at birth, this king changed his name as a sign of his monotheistic beliefs ("Akhenaten" meant "the one who serves Aten," the sun god, which he considered to be *the only* god). His religious shift marked an interesting (albeit short-lived) era in Egyptian religion, as King Akhenaten made the entirety of Egypt follow his monotheistic beliefs. After his death, Egypt reclaimed their old, polytheistic beliefs back.

It would also be quite interesting to mention that King Akhenaten's wife was none other than the famous Nefertiti. This might surprise you, but she was not an actual Queen of Egypt (although some believe she ruled as Neferneferuaten after her husband's death and before the rise of King Tutankhamun).

Together, Akhenaten and Nefertiti ruled through one of the most prosperous ages of Egypt.

King Tutankhamun

Perhaps the pharaoh's name on everyone's lips, King Tutankhamun's life was far less notable than his death (or, better said, *after-death*). He came to ruling when he was only 10, and passed away when he was 20. However, what he is most famous for is his grave, which was discovered as absolutely intact to many archeologists' surprise (who, by 1922, when this happened, had kind of gotten used to Egyptian tombs being entirely robbed out).

King Ramses II

Ramses II, also known as King Ramses the Great, was an ostentatious ruler (even by Egyptian standards, which pretty much meant decades of work put into building one's *grave*, literally). King Ramses II had a great contribution to the growth and consolidation of Egypt's economy. He also had quite a lot of time to do this, as he ruled for no less than 67 years (time in which he also declared himself a God). During this time, it is believed that he fathered no less than 96 children (which might be the "seed" that set out to crumble the Egyptian Empire from within just a couple of generations later).

Queen Cleopatra VII

Everyone knows about Cleopatra, but most people know about her through the prism of her involvement with Romans Caesar and Marc Anthony. She is known to have been a great seductress and an agile politician who fought to maintain peace and prosperity in Egypt. However, her death by suicide in 30 BC, came to represent the death of the Egyptian Empire itself.

You see, *Game of Thrones* has nothing on the intricacies, wars, and internal battles Egyptian dynasties fought for thousands of years. From Queen Regents who take over and become pharaohs to kings and queens who are direct descendants of the gods and mysteries of tombs that were miraculously intact until their discovery in the 20th century, Ancient Egypt has it all: drama, love stories, women fighting for the throne, massive buildings, death, and pain.

The rise and fall of the Egyptian Empire remain somewhat shrouded in mystery for many reasons. Fortunately, however, dated historical facts and archeology help us determine the course of things in Ancient Egypt—and, as you will probably notice later on in this book, they are *a lot* easier to understand than the mysteries that continue to fuel a world's imagination.

Before we dive into that, however, let's take some time to talk about an element of Ancient Egypt that is just as fascinating as its history: Egyptian culture.

Chapter 2: Egyptian Culture

Bar from the whole "pharaohs are actually gods" part and several other twists and turns Egyptian history took over time; it can be said that the flow of Egyptian history is quite straightforward. Allright, it did have its fair share of intrigue and mystery. But overall, historians and egyptologists have plenty of sources to retrace the rise and fall of Ancient Egypt, factually speaking.

Egyptian culture, however, is a little more complex. On the one hand, Egyptian culture was heavily influenced by the Nile River (I really wasn't joking when I said the life of the entire empire revolved around this river). The influence of the Nile is so great on the entire civilization of the Egyptians that it can be easily said that Ancient Egyptians would have simply *not existed* if it weren't for this river.

This does make sense. In a desert area with a very hot climate, the Nile River was, indeed, a gift—one that allowed Egypt to flourish not only from an agricultural point of view but from a cultural and technological perspective too.

On the other hand, the myths, legends, and shifting spirituality of Egyptians also had a heavy impact on their cultural development. Of course, much of the Egyptian technology cannot be fully explained to the date, but looking into their myths and the art that resulted from them can give us an idea of how Egyptians *really* lived.

And that is what we aim to do in this chapter: take an honest, high-level look at Egypt's culture, both from an artistic and linguistic perspective and from a technological point of view.

Ancient Egypt's Language

Most people associate Egypt with hieroglyphic writing, and, for the largest part, that is a pretty correct assumption.

Egyptologists divide the evolution of the Egyptian language into five main categories (Hoch, n.d.):

- Old Egyptian
- Middle Egyptian
- Late Egyptian
- Demotic
- Coptic

It is worth mentioning that all these language periods refer to the written language (since it is the one we can reconstruct the best, given how long it has been since it was used). Spoken language is believed to have differed quite a lot from the written version.

Of all these versions, the Coptic language is considered to be the latest, and it is still used in religious rituals by Egyptian Christians. Other than that, however, Egyptian as a language is considered to be extinct.

The Egyptian language was written in hieroglyphics, that is true. However, that was just one of the three main types of writing styles adopted by Egyptians throughout history. Aside from it, there were also Hieratic and Demotic writing on papyruses, and, later on, Coptic came to use as well. Coptic alphabet was mostly based on the Greek alphabet, and it was used mostly in religious texts (or, at least, the texts that have survived until now are religious in nature).

How Did Hieroglyphic Writing "Work"?

The first Egyptian hieroglyphs were found on pottery jars and ivory plaques in Egyptian tombs, dating as far back as 4,000 BCE. Back then, these hieroglyphs were mostly used to identify the dead. Later on, the same writing system started to be used on monuments and tomb walls. Their purpose was to identify the "sponsor" of the monument or the one buried in the tomb, but also to make an account of their lives (hunting expeditions, great deeds, wars, and other notable events) (Brunner, n.d.).

Indeed, looking at what Egyptians left behind in terms of writing can be mesmerizing because every little symbol feels like it pertains to a near-magical world.

Hieroglyphic writing was quite straight-forward and aside from the meanings it conveyed, there's not much magical about it. Basically, every character in the hieroglyphic writing was represented through a picture. Each of them could be read as pictures, symbols for pictures, or as symbols for certain sounds.

The word "hieroglyphic" comes from Greek, and it literally means "sacred writing" (based on what Greeks noticed when they came in contact with the Egyptians). Furthermore, Greeks also distinguished from the two other types of writing Egyptians used, especially since hieroglyphic writing only appeared on walls (particularly temple walls), while Hieratic and Demotic texts were written on papyruses.

Initially, "hieroglyphic writing" was only used to describe Egyptian writing on walls. But in the late 19th century, it started to be associated with all similar forms of writing (which used pictures as characters). Such writing systems include Mayan and Incan, Hittite, and the writings found on Easter Island.

Art, Music, and Literature in Ancient Egypt

If you stop to look at any artifact dating from Ancient Egypt, you will notice that, for thousands of years, Egyptians really did have an appetite for beauty. There is something uniquely lavish in their burial sites and monuments, and there is nothing quite like it throughout the entirety of the Ancient world.

Clearly, Egyptians did appreciate art, but in most situations, art played a more practical role than what we acknowledge it today (Mark, 2017). Plastic arts were systematized. They were almost like a design system where every single symbol has a very clear meaning and way of being drawn (it makes sense since this was used not "just" for aesthetic purposes, but also to write down history and communicate messages).

Of course, you definitely imagined Egyptians were into plastic arts. Pretty much everything we have left from them points in that direction. But did you ever imagine Egyptians listening to music?

Because they did. Although it might not be to modern taste, historians say that Egyptians did have music in their culture. Even more than that, they had quite a lot of instruments, including percussion (such as rattles, hand-held drums, and the sistrum, an instrument used in religious rituals), wind (flutes and trumpets), and string instruments (such as harps and lyres, for example).

Music was mostly associated with religious rites in Ancient Egypt, and it was included in worship rituals that were meant for childbirth and fertility as well. Even more, the original belly dance is believed to have been born in Egypt, too (Fraser, 2014).

Judging by what an essential role death and mortuary rituals played in the lives of Egyptians, it might also make quite a lot of sense to you to learn that most of Ancient Egypt's literature revolved around, well, *death*. There are accounts of autobiographies and hymns, but most of them revolved around the afterlife and what it meant for the pharaohs (Mark, 2016).

All in all, Egyptians did love art, but they probably had a very different definition of it than what we have today. Emotions, perspectives, and stories were reserved to the lives and deaths for the pharaohs and, occasionally, retellings of myths and legends (of which, of course, pharaohs were part of as direct descendants or even corporeal representations of the gods themselves).

We can only imagine what the average Egyptian listened to or what kind of art they were surrounded by. Unfortunately, there is not enough evidence to point to how everyone else other than the royals lived their lives and died their deaths (in a manner of speaking, of course).

Ancient's Egypt's Burial Rites

As you have probably noticed (or at least guessed), Egyptians were quite big on the idea of death. Pharaohs and royals were buried with entire fortunes, and sometimes, as morbid as it might seem, they took their loved ones with them (and that included their pets as well) (Mark, 2013).

What is the deal with all this, though? How is it that Ancient Egypt revolved so much around death and the mortuary? Even pharaohs, supposedly super-human to some extent at least, centered their entire lives around the idea of death (that's why they built so many pyramids, temples, and mortuary sites, after all).

To understand Egyptian burial customs, you should first understand that their idea of "afterlife" was quite different than ours. While people in Western cultures imagine the afterlife to be a more or less abstract concept, for the Egyptians, the afterlife was merely a continuation of their lives on Earth.

That explains why they took everything with them in death, as it had followed them in life. From riches to beloved, they wanted everything that made their lives happy in *this* life to be transported to the next one.

The earliest burial rites date as far back as 6,000 BCE, which points to the fact that, throughout the entire duration of the Egyptian culture, they were quite close to the idea of the afterlife and what it represents.

Eternity was the final destination of every Egyptian, regardless of gender or age. And what might seem interesting is that, although the land of the afterlife was a land of bliss, Egyptians did mourn their dead (and quite dramatically so, if I may add).

The reason Egyptians mummified their bodies is related precisely to this: they wanted to preserve their physical bodies for as long as possible. There was also multiple types of mummification "available," each in their own price category:

- The most expensive type of mummification involved using not only "divine salts" (a mixture of different sodiums) but also removing the brain from the body

through the nostrils and keeping the body in a special embalming mixture for longer periods of time.
- The second most expensive type of mummification was similar to the first, but less attention was given to the body, and the dead person was returned to their family without much ceremony
- The least expensive type of mummification involved keeping the body in an embalming solution for seven days only, without any kind of attention given to ceremonial practices.

In all these cases, the organs were removed from the body. However, since Egyptians believed the heart was connected to the soul, they left it in the body. They also kept the viscera because they believed the dead would need it in the afterlife.

All Egyptians, regardless of social status, took mummification *very* seriously. They also believed that someone who was not properly mummified was to return as a ghost (and this is something they literally lived their lives for). The poorest Egyptians gave their old clothes to be used in wrapping the dead body, and all burial sites included at least some sort of collection of belongings from the dead person (and yes, even the poorer Egyptians did that).

As mentioned above, life and death were intrinsically connected to Egyptians. In life, every Egyptian was called to work on a construction project for a given amount of time. If they were ill or could not attend their civic duties, they had the right to send a replacement worker once a year. In death, Egyptians place "shabti dolls" in their graves because they believed they would have to perform the same civic duty in the afterlife, and these dolls were meant to be their replacement dolls. As such, almost every grave included one of these.

Lamentation was also part of the burial rite. No matter how popular someone was, everyone hired "professional" lamenters to mourn and sing special songs at someone's burial. For Ancient Egyptians, this was simply a way to remember the dead (but they actually *did* believe the dead person was heading to a better place).

In many ways, Ancient Egyptians were very much similar to us when it comes to death. In most ways, however, their death and funeral rites are at least part of why everyone is so fascinated with their culture today.

Death and life were part of the same game, and they were always intertwined with the lives of the gods and their teachings (or cautionary tales). For Ancient Egyptians, death was just a "next stage," and they dedicated their entire lives to it.

Science and Technology in Ancient Egypt

The other major reason we are all so fascinated with Ancient Egypt is, of course, their level of science and technology.

Pyramids are, perhaps, one of the most intriguing topics related to the science and technology Egyptians possessed. We will, however, talk more about this in Chapter 3 of this book.

Aside from that, Egyptians paid a lot of attention to their technology and how they passed along their knowledge. The Library of Alexandria is, without a doubt, one of the most impressive collections of knowledge in the entire Ancient world (and although it was built towards the end of Ancient Egypt as a whole, most historians associate it with that period).

Not only were Egyptians great builders (quite obviously so, considering their structures survived thousands of years and they are still very much a mystery), but they were also great agriculturers. For example, they had intricate irrigation systems that ensured their beloved Nile River would feed all the areas that needed growth (White, 2003).

Moreover, accounts of medicine and astronomy are also connected to Ancient Egypt , showing that they were not only into engineering but also in other sciences. Of course, much of their astronomy was connected to their deities, but their observations played a role in painting the world of the ancients.

As for medicine, Egyptians are known to have created one of the first medical treaties in neuroscience (the Edwin Smith Papyrus, discovered in the 19th century, which analyzed trauma and how the brain reacted to it) (Wilkins, 1992).

The Egyptians might not have invented the wheel in the sense of how we imagine it today; however, they are considered to be early adopters of the potters' wheels previously invented in Mesopotamia (Bellis, 2019). And even though the Hyksos are largely attributed to having been the first to use the chariot wheel (one of their military *fortes*, actually), Egyptians were early adopters when it came to that as well.

Ancient Egypt is mysterious and fascinating at the same time, and all this is largely due to how they managed to create buildings and engineer systems well ahead of their time. This goes to show that, although divinity, life, and death were the ones to rule supreme over Egyptians' lives, they also paid quite a lot of attention to how well they lived their lives and strived to make constant improvements on the quality of it.

Interesting Facts about Egyptian Culture

A people's culture always transpires well beyond the simple categories (art, religion, science, and technology). Sometimes, the most pervasive, interesting, and revealing things about a nation's culture lie in the small things. Like, for example, how women did their hair, what people wore, and how the daily life of a person pertaining to that nation and era went by.

For this reason, I choose to end the second chapter of this book with a quick list of things that are quite interesting when it comes to Ancient Egyptian culture:

The Calendar

It is believed that the 365-day calendar was invented by Egyptians roughly 5,000 years ago. The reason they created this calendar was to follow the rise and fall of the Nile River (and thus, plan their agricultural activities according to this) (Ancient Egypt Online, n.d.)

Makeup and Beauty

In Ancient Egypt, both men and women wore makeup. Aside from the aesthetic purposes of doing this, makeup also had a functional role: protect the eyes from the sunlight. Kohl was applied to the eyelids similarly to the "cat-eye" makeup today. Eye makeup was essential in Ancient Egypt, as it protected

Egyptians not only from the glare of the sun, but it was also believed to have healing properties (mostly because it was antibacterial and it combined with the moisture on the eyelid skin).

Furthermore, Egyptians also wore a layer of green eye makeup derived from copper. And if that might surprise you, they also wore red paint on their lips (which was often made from highly toxic ingredients).

Ancient Egyptians also took care of their skin quite a lot. For instance, milk and honey treatments were very popular (and they are still today, as many beauty products include these ingredients) (Wolkoff, 2020).

Cats and Pets

Much like the internet today, Ancient Egyptians also loved cats. In fact, they revered them to the point where they considered them sacred (and even "took" them in their afterlife) (Brogan, 2017).

Not only did Ancient Egyptians love cats, but they also kept quite a wide range of other pets around their homes. They had dogs, baboons, birds, lions, monkeys, and even hippopotamuses as their pets (Mark, 2016). King Tut is believed to have been killed by a hippo (which he was most likely attempting to hunt) (Andrews, 2020).

Entertainment

Thought board games are a new invention? Think again, it seems that Egyptians also found plenty of time to play around in between building world-class structures. Senet is considered to be one of the oldest "board" games in the history of mankind and, much like our board games today, it involved throwing sticks to see how many moves one must make (just like we throw the dice today) (Discovering Egypt, n.d.).

Cleopatra

Cleopatra might be one of the most preeminent feminine figures of the Ancient World, and she most definitely ruled Egypt, but she was not Egyptian per se. In fact, she was Macedonian Greek (as, by then, Egypt had already been conquered by Alexander the Great and a Greek dynasty was ruling over the country) (San Jose State University, n.d.).

War and Peace

Ancient Egyptians are credited to have created one of the oldest peace treatises in the world. It seems that, aside from being super-concerned with building tombs for their deaths (and sometimes going to war to have the financial resources for that), Egyptians also had more peaceful and earthly thoughts. In the second millennia BCE, perhaps tired from all the fighting for two centuries, Egyptians forged a peace treaty with the Hittites (inhabitants of what is roughly today considered to be Syria) (Andrews, 2020).

Freedom for Women

Egyptian women enjoyed quite a lot of freedom. They could enter legal contracts, buy and sell, and even work outside of the home. Unlike many women today, they also received equal pay for their work outside of the home. And even more than that, unlike Greek women, they were also allowed to divorce, remarry, and create prenuptial contracts. Yes, they were viewed as inferior to men, but with all this, they still enjoyed a lot of freedom, especially for that age (Andrews, 2020).

Beer

Egyptians drank beer. OK, it was not the beer we know today, but even so, it was the closest thing to a modern beer you could get. The way they made beer was by leaving loaves of bread in heated jars to ferment. They also added honey and dates for taste and sweetness, so this drink might not be to the modern beer drinker's taste. Nevertheless, Egyptians enjoyed it quite a lot, to the point where many pharaohs are believed to have been quite overweight (because beer, bread, honey, and wine are *never* good on a waistline, right?) (Mark, 2017; Andrews, 2020).

Ancient Egyptians (and much of the Ancient world, actually) were surprisingly similar to us. From their passions to their pets, it seems that their culture was a very advanced one—much like ours today. In the following chapter, we will talk more about Egyptian pyramids and everything they represented, as both flagships of Ancient Egyptian culture *and* as a mystery of our modern understanding of them.

Chapter 3: Egyptian Pyramids & Treasures

Few artifacts of the ancient world make the modern world as fascinated as pyramids, and Egyptian treasures do. From very young kids to reputable scholars, Egyptian fascination seems to have a hold on pretty much everyone, regardless of age, social status, or origins.

Egyptian pyramids are, indeed, quite the mystery. You have all the reasons to be fascinated with these intriguing structures, with everything they hide, and everything they represent for the Ancient Egyptians.

In this chapter, we will try to discover some of the most interesting facts about Egyptian pyramids and the treasures they held, from meaning and symbolism to building technology and how these pyramids were discovered by the modern world.

Ancient Egyptian Pyramids: A Tale of Perfection

One of the main reasons pyramids are such a great source of fascination and why they have fed our imagination for so long is precisely their perfection (and *how* exactly did ancient people manage to nail the engineering and building techniques of constructions of such an amplitude).

For most people, the words "Ancient Egyptian pyramids" are somewhat synonymous with the famous pyramids located on the Giza. It's easy to understand why: the Giza pyramids are, in truth, absolutely mesmerizing. Perfect, down to the smallest rock and limestone piece included in their build, these pyramids are both works of art and masterpieces of construction, architecture, and technology.

Not all pyramids look just like that, though. It is believed there are approximately 138 (Slackman, 2008) pyramids in Egypt and, although the ones at Giza are essential to our understanding of Egyptian history and culture, the other ones are equally important too. Even more, looking at older pyramids can help us understand how the "miracles" on the Giza plateau came to be (and no, I promise, no alien theories are involved here).

As noted in the first chapter, the first recorded pyramid is the one built for King Djoser. This is, of course, the first *step* pyramid recorded in Egypt, but similar structures were actually used long before Djoser, and they were called "mastaba." There are visible differences between any pyramid you would imagine and these mastabas, as the latter were inward sloping burial structures with a flat roof.

Both the sloping structure and the flat roof had powerful symbolic meaning for the way the deceased would pave their way to the afterlife. For example, the sloping structure was meant to help the dead climb their way to the sun. The very evolution of how pyramids looked is quite tightly connected to this structure because the smoother the surface of the pyramid appeared, the easier it was for the deceased to find their way upwards.

It is believed that King Djoser's pyramid also began as a simple mastaba but evolved into a much more ambitious project—and hence, the first step pyramid in the history of Egypt was born.

Later on, multiple other pyramids were built, but none is as famous as the ones at Giza. Built for King Snerfu, Khufu, and Menkaure, these pyramids have been standing tall, guarding over Cairo's outskirts, for thousands of years.

They didn't just start building smooth-surfaced pyramids right away. It is believed that King Snerfu (the one who built the first of the three pyramids of Giza) made several failed attempts before proceeding with the first structure on the Giza plateau.

The largest of the three Great Pyramids of Giza was built for his son, King Khufu. Ironically, he wanted his pyramid to help his name survive for 4,500 years and be a mega-structure that would speak about his grandeur. However the only representation of him as a king in the entire pyramid is a very small statue of several inches.

The third of the pyramids of Giza was created for Menkaure (but commissioned by his father, Khafre). This is the smallest pyramid of the three, but it is in no way less impressive. Together with the other two, Menkaure's pyramid points to Heliopolis, where the Temple of Re was located, adding even more meaning and symbolism to the entire structure.

All of the pyramids were meant to offer their "owners" a comfortable, happy afterlife. Aside from the tomb itself, many of them included entire rooms meant for different activities, and even a small door the deceased soul could use to move in and out of their burial room.

Many other pyramids are sprinkled throughout Egypt, testimonies of a culture that believed that life is just another step to lead to, well, death—just like the steps of the first pyramids were meant to lead to the plateau on top. (Parra, n,d; Smithsonian, n.d; History.com, 2019).

The Mystery of the Pyramids

Not only are pyramids fascinating in their grandeur and everything they symbolize (they are, the fact of the matter speaking, very, very large tombs, after all). They are also fascinating because we still cannot fully understand how Ancient Egyptians managed to pull off these architectural miracles even with all our technology and knowledge.

The word "miracle" is not lightly used here, especially considering they happened when neither knowledge nor technology was *that* advanced (let us not forget the Hyksos chariot came as a massive surprise and a breakthrough technological development at that time).

The main question egyptologists have about building the pyramids is related to how exactly they managed to transport the limestone blocks (and how they managed to pull them to the great heights of the largest pyramids).

More specifically, it is estimated that more than two million limestone blocks were used in erecting the Cheops Pyramid. Given that these limestone blocks are believed to have been sourced at a significant distance from the pyramid and given that pulling them up might have been troublesome, scientists today are still wondering how Egyptians managed to do all this (Stewart, 2018).

The secrets of the pyramid building techniques came closer to an end just a couple of short years ago when we found evidence that Egyptians might have used a ramp with stairs to carry the blocks to the highest points of the pyramids (Rawlinson, 2018). Things are still pretty uncertain, though, leaving room for all sorts of conspiracies to shape up (including that aliens visited the Egyptians and gave them the technology they needed).

Another interesting mystery about the pyramids is related to the interiors of these super-tombs. More exactly, it was discovered (quite recently) that some of the pyramids had "voids" inside—rooms that don't appear to have served any purpose, but which seem to appear in multiple pyramids, built at considerable years apart from each other (Greshko, 2017).

Furthermore, what might be even more baffling is that the Great Pyramid of Giza can tell time. It is known that Egyptians used astronomy in building these structures, but it is not yet known why they decided this specific pyramid should act like a massive sundial (its shadow can tell time quite precisely, at different points in the day) (Greskho, 2017).

Last but not least, one of the greatest pyramid-related mysteries is also related to how other civilizations located extremely far away from the Egyptians managed to build their own pyramids.

Aztecs and Mayans had stepped pyramids; China, Indonesia, and Cambodia had pyramids too. The resemblances between these structures and the Egyptian ones are, in truth, quite amazing, especially when you consider the fact that these cultures did not "communicate" with each other (or at least not that we know of).

There are many other mysteries and urban legends surrounding the built, purpose, and survival of the pyramids of Egypt. It is, of course, pretty easy to give in to all sorts of conspiracies when it comes to structures as baffling and as awe-inspiring as the pyramids.

In reality, however, it is highly unlikely that any of these pyramids and temples were *that* mysterious. Our entire view of how civilizations evolved (and fell) is rather skewed. We always imagine getting to this point of technological advancement was more of a steadily upwards slope, but in fact, it was a *wavy* one. Civilizations rose and fell, and with them, the technology they used.

To make a parenthesis in this direction, Ancient Rome had a very good idea of how to build aqueducts, but by the time Vikings were invading the nowadays territory of the UK (which had been colonized by Romans), nobody had any idea of how Romans did it.

The case of the pyramids could very much be like that. Just because Egyptians had the knowledge to build them and then everyone "forgot" how to do it, it really does not mean there's any conspiracy at play.

It just means we have an improper understanding of how civilizations "work".

Either way you look at it, though, the Egyptian pyramids are highly fascinating and definitely (still very much) worth our attention. Our imagination can run as wild as we want to, but the facts remained the same: we don't know much about them, but the Egyptian pyramids will continue to inspire, thrill, and animate our wildest thoughts.

The Ancient Egyptian Mummification Process

Next to the pyramids, the Ancient Egyptian mummification process is one of the main reasons so many people feel an almost unbeatable attraction towards Ancient Egyptian culture.

Mummies have stirred creativity and imagination for quite some time. The first Egyptian mummy was discovered towards the end of the 19th century (Oldest.org, n.d.), when stories of the exotic and esoteric were flooding the entire Victorian space. Thus, it comes as no surprise that the very beginning of how we see mummies is associated with a lot of mystery.

In time, we came to understand a lot more about the Egyptian mummification processes and the reasons behind all the effort they put into doing this (as mentioned in the previous chapter, it was a heavily religious ritual).

It is worth noting that mummification was not an exclusively Egyptian practice (Leveille, 2015). The oldest mummy ever found was located in Chile, and it was dated 6,000 years ago. While it might be true that Egyptians have practiced mummification for a very long time, the ultimate truth is that we don't know if they were the first ones to do it. And they most certainly are not the last, as mummies were discovered outside of Egypt, long after the end of the Empire.

Some of the most famous Egyptian mummies include the following:

King Tutankhamon's Mummy

By far, one of the single most well-known mummies in the world, King Tut's dead body, is the reason we have the "mummy curse" legend. Discovered in 1922 by Howard Carter, this mummy is considered to be one of the main reasons so many people are fascinated with Egyptology (India Today, 2016).

It's easy to understand why, after all.

King Tutankhamon's tomb was the only one we have discovered that seemed to be almost entirely untouched. This would lead one to believe there was something supposedly strong to protect it. However, later discoveries pointed out that it was the location of the tomb (underneath workmen's tombs) that protected it from robberies. Furthermore, it seems that King Tut's tomb *was* robbed, but it was also resealed twice.

To add to the mystery, Lord Carnavon, the man who financed Howard Carter's expedition to Egypt, died of a mysterious mosquito bite just months after the uncovering of King Tut's tomb.

On top of all that, it seems that most egyptologists are quite baffled because this specific tomb was much smaller than other pharaohs. This might signal that King Tutankhamon died unexpectedly, and as such, a previously built tomb had to be repurposed for him. (Zorich, 2016)

Furthermore, it seems that other bodies were buried with him. Some archeologists are optimistic enough to believe one of the bodies might pertain to none other than Nefertiti.

The cause of death, as well as whose son Tutankhamon actually was (and who followed him on the throne of Egypt)—there are plenty of mysteries surrounding this mummy. Obviously, nothing is absolutely certain when it comes to King Tutankhamon's body and tomb. However, what *is* certain is that he will continue to fuel many people's imagination for a long time from now on.

Ramses II's Body

As mentioned earlier in the book, this was one of the greatest kings of Egypt. He lived for more than 90 years, and it is believed that he fathered nearly 100 children. Furthermore, he has a long list of achievements to his "resume." This might also be why, when his mummy was flown to France to be treated for a fungal infection, he even received a modern Egyptian passport citing his occupation as "King (deceased)." Allright, that was not the reason why; it was merely a legislative requirement in Egypt in the 1970s, so authorities compiled—but it is quite interesting to think of a passport issued no less than 3,000 years after its owner's death.

Hatshepsut's Mummy

Hatshepsut's reign was rather scandalous (because, well, she was the first woman to rule over Egypt. She was also basically ruling on behalf of her stepson, who came to pretty much erasing her from history after he came to the throne). She was discovered in 1902 by the same Howard Carter, who uncovered King Tut's tomb. However, her mummy was not identified until much later on when one of her teeth (preserved separately from the body) helped archeologists connect the dots and confirm it was her (Pilkington, 2007).

Ginger

Archeologists are not entirely sure who "Ginger" is (they nicknamed the mummy after its red hair). However, he is most definitely one of the most famous ones in the world. Together with the other mummies discovered at the same site, Ginger is the oldest one of its kind in Egypt (dating to 3,400 BCE.). He is also the first mummy ever to be displayed in a museum (he's been at the British Museum since 1901).

The Golden Mummies

Although they are not necessarily associated with pharaohs, the Golden Mummies discovered in 1996 in Egypt's Western Desert are fascinating because they seem to cover every social stratum you could imagine: from wealthy merchants to poorer locals.

Nefertiti

I will call this the "most famous mummy in absentia" because, to the date, it has not been determined if Nefertiti's mummy was actually found. The latest news shows that some egyptologists are positive that Nefertiti's mummy is one of two other unidentified mummies that have already been discovered. (Marie, 2019).

These are, of course, just some of the most commonly known Egyptian mummies in the world. Many others were uncovered, and there is a very high likelihood that many others *will* be uncovered from hereon as well.

From mummies coming back to life in Hollywood movies to mummies being displayed in museums, there is a nearly crazy wide range of stories surrounding the process of mummification and its purposes. We are yet to see what stories *"new"* mummies will fuel in the future.

The Ancient Egyptian Treasures and Their Fascination

There is no doubt we're fascinated with the pyramids and the mummies uncovered in Egypt. Another source of great interest is represented by the Egyptian treasures, most of which were found buried with the aforementioned mummies.

It would take entire books to list and talk about some of the most amazing treasures and discoveries egyptologists have made over the past two centuries, but unfortunately, this is not the scope of this book.

I do, however, want to introduce you to some of the most stunning treasures uncovered around Egypt:

- **The Rosetta Stone**. This carved stone is an essential discovery for egyptologists (and the world as a whole). Although it might not seem like much, this stone is the reason we finally managed to understand hieroglyphic writing. Written for King Ptolemy V to state his right to rule over Egypt, the Rosetta Stone's contents were carved down in three languages: hieroglyphic, demotic, and Greek. This helped linguists gain a better understanding of hieroglyphic writing. (Pruitt, 2019)

- **Khufu's Ship**. Uncovered at the base of Khufu's pyramid, this ship is a prime example of Egyptian navigation (which, by the way, they were quite apt in). Today, this ship is on display at the Solar Boat Museum, a place built at Giza, especially to showcase this important artifact of the ancient world.

- **The Silver Pharaoh**. At the beginning of World War II, Pierre Montet discovered a tomb that rivaled that of Tutankhamon in terms of the kinds of riches it contained. Among other things discovered in the tomb, the most shocking item was the sarcophagus itself. This sarcophagus made egyptologists question their knowledge because it was made entirely out of silver, and with a stunning burial mask made from gold. The tomb belonged to King Psusennes, a pretty unknown pharaoh of Ancient Egypt who was mostly associated with an era when Egypt was not very influential or well-off (according to what historians believed before the discovery of this tomb). However, judging by the treasures discovered here, archeologists and historians were forced to reconsider their understanding of Egypt's different periods.

Of course, many other treasures and artifacts were uncovered. Some bear a very high material price (such as those that are made from gold or silver). Others are precious at a more spiritual and intellectual level because they help us understand more about Ancient Egyptians. Though, each of them is important as it is a testimony of a glorious past we are yet to fully comprehend.

Famous Ancient Egyptian Temples and Pyramids

Along with pyramids and other fascinating structures (such as the Sphinx of Giza, for example), Ancient Egyptian temples are a great source of interest for laypeople and egyptologists alike.

Egypt is sprinkled with many such temples. Pretty much everywhere you turn, in every location around the country, you are likely to find at least one amazing temple or pyramid in the nearby region.

We have already discussed pyramids quite extensively, so in this part of Chapter 3, we will only list down some of the most popular ones. However, I will mention temples, as it will be relevant for the following chapters of the book as well. More specifically, it is important to note that not all Ancient Egyptian temples are quite the same. As a general rule, egyptologists have determined there are three main temple categories:

- Classical (which are dedicated to one specific God)
- Mortuary (dedicated to a pharaoh)
- Solar (dedicated to the Sun God Ra, and built in a way that reflects the sun rays)

Some of the most appreciated Ancient Egyptian temples and pyramids include the following:

The Pyramids of Giza

Without a doubt the most famous pyramids in all Egypt, the Giza pyramids are fascinating for their structure, architecture, and size. Built between 3575 and 3170 BCE, they now represent one of the main tourist destinations in all of Egypt—and for all good reasons.

The Luxor Temple

Amenophis III started this temple but it was only finished during Ramses II's reign. It is a truly awe-inspiring architectural beauty dedicated to Amon-Ra, featuring two seated statues of Ramses that are more than 15-meters high, as well as several statues of prisoners representing all the nations Egypt ruled over. What is interesting is that many other pharaohs that succeeded Ramses II also tried to leave their mark on the Luxor. In fact, it is believed that even the "boy king" Tutankhamon and Alexander the Great wanted to be immortalized at Luxor.

The Temple of Horus at Edfu

Dedicated to the sky god Horus, this temple is one of the most amazing historical sites ever discovered in Egypt. The reason behind its importance lies in its hieroglyphs. Not only are there *plenty* of them in this temple, but they have also been preserved quite well, which has given historians plenty of sources to help with the "reconstruction" of Ancient Egypt's past.

The Temples at Kom el-Sultan

Kom el-Sultan hosts three very important temples: the temple of Seti I, the temple of Ramses II, and the Abydos temple. Of the three, the Abydos temple is believed to be the oldest (dating from the First Dynasty). Unfortunately, it has not been preserved very well (although some of the decorative reliefs are easily noticeable even today).

Pyramid of Lahun

This pyramid, built around 1180 BCE., is fascinating because it looks like no other pyramid ever found in Egypt. It has not been preserved very well, and all its interiors are now inaccessible, but everything found inside (as well as the buried village next to it) was used by historians to understand Egypt at that time better.

The Pyramid of Meidum

Some Egyptologists consider this to be only a "pseudo pyramid" because its construction is not similar to the step pyramid at Saqqara, nor to the other steeply inclined pyramids (such as the one at Giza). It is clear that, at the point when Meidum was built, Egyptians hadn't exactly nailed the science of erecting pyramids—but that makes this specific one even more fascinating.

The Bent Pyramid at Dahshur

This pyramid also has an atypical shape (more specifically, its base and its upper side are inclined at different angles, giving it a very dissimilar structure to all the other pyramids).

Along with all the other pyramids, temples, and structures already discussed in these introductory chapters, the ones mentioned here represent the rise and fall of the Egyptian Empire. In the end, however, pyramids, temples, and even mummies are nothing but earthly remains of that civilization. The real catalyst behind all of it was, in fact, Egyptian spirituality and religion.

In Chapter 4 and 5, we will dive a little deeper into the stories of gods and goddesses of Ancient Egypt, how they formed a culture, and, ultimately, how their legends survived to the modern-day.

Chapter 4: Famous Egyptian Myths

As discussed in previous chapters, death played an essential role in every Egyptian's life. It sounds paradoxical, but all evidence shows that Egyptians were people who lived their lives, not only being very aware of their death one day but also preparing for it. Sometimes, they did so by building exceedingly intricate structures to help them have a better afterlife.

This entire view on life was heavily influenced by their legends and myths. A polytheistic society (bar from a short period of time when monotheism was imposed on them), Egypt's religion shifted and changed over time. Just like in Ancient Greece, Egyptians shifted interest from one god to another, but for the vast majority of the time, the myths surrounding these gods and goddesses stayed the same.

These are more than just mere stories. They are meaningful down to every word. They have the power to show us what Egyptians really lived like, how they understood life and its major events, and how they were looking at the Cosmos, at natural events, and everything that was not yet fully explained.

In this chapter, we will discuss some of the most important myths and legends of Ancient Egypt's gods and goddesses, focusing on how these stories shaped their civilization and culture.

We will start with a short introduction to mythology in general, as I believe it is quite important for you to understand the real meaning of the word "myth" and its function in developing a civilization. Once that is out of the way, we will dive right into the mythic stories of the lives of Ancient Egyptians.

Myths - A Gate to the Unknown

Myths lie at the very foundation of civilization. All the great cultures in history are known to have had their own fair share of mythology. Greeks had their own, Romans had their own (and they also kind of "borrowed" some from the Greeks), Mesopotamians had their own, and Slavs had their own. It is likely that the first people to settle in the territories of Indo-Europe also had their own myths.

According to Dictionary.com (2020), a myth is

> "a traditional or legendary story, usually concerning some being or hero or event, with or without a determinable basis of fact or a natural explanation, especially one that is concerned with deities or demigods and explains some practice, rite, or phenomenon of nature."

To this definition, it must also be added that myths have consistently contributed to shaping up entire cultures. Even more, they lie at the foundation of philosophical movements, religions, and sometimes even politics (especially in theocratic states).

Myths are more than just stories. They transcend through everything that comes their way. They are not science; they rarely explain natural phenomena as they are, and they can be quite dangerous when people are too fervent about them. And yet, myths are an essential *need* human beings have been having ever since the beginning of time.

Joseph Campbell puts this very well in discussion with Bill Moyers (Moyers, 1988):

> *"Myth is a manifestation in symbolic images, metaphorical images, of the energies within us, moved by the organs of the body, in conflict with each other. This organ wants this; this organ wants this: the brain is one of the organs."*

Not only is this very aptly put, but it also manages to encompass a more realistic definition of myths and what they truly represent for human beings. Myths can bring down kingdoms and influence nations. They can move armies and touch our emotions, and they can inspire as much as they can dishearten.

The rise and fall of different cultures are strongly connected to their myths, and not just in the Ancient world. Again, Joseph Campbell speaks about this quite eloquently in his book, *The Hero with a Thousand Faces*. Here, he argues that human beings have always searched for defining myths. From the myths of Ancient Egypt to modern-day myths like that of Luke Skywalker in *Star Wars*, these stories have given hope, have put people down, and they have influenced our lives in ways we are not even fully aware of (Campbell, 2008).

In this chapter, we will talk a little about some of the most famous stories and myths of Ancient Egypt, as well as how they can be interpreted (at least from a limited perspective, as it would take, again, entire libraries full of books to run through all the perspectives Egyptian myths can encompass).

Genesis and the High-Level Stories of the Egyptian Mythology

To understand the story of Ra and all the other Egyptian gods, you have first to understand how the world was created according to Egyptians. As you will see, the genesis story of the world Egyptians came up with is not that much different from that which is encountered in any of the major monotheistic religions today (namely, Judaism, Christianity, and Islam).

Egyptians believed that, before *anything* existed, *nothing* did. They thought darkness was floating through the Primeval Ocean. Only Atum, the entity that ruled supreme over the nothingness, would be able to decide when creation begins—and so he did, when the breath of life was strong enough.

And so Ra came to exist. The god of the sun for Ancient Egyptians was born on an island that emerged in the water. He then created the first gods: Shu (representing Dryness and Air) and Tefnut (representing Humidity).

From here on, other gods came to be. At first, Geb (representing Earth) and Nut (representing the Sky) came to life. They gave birth to what Egyptians called the "Principles of Life" (Osiris, the Perfect Being).

And while all this was happening, Ra was creating the human world by naming each of the elements. Osiris was meant to rule supreme over Earth, and he started off by teaching humans how to grow their own food and how to build civilization.

Osiris also had a mate (who was, perhaps oddly for us today, also his sister): Isis. She was "in charge" with magic and creativity and completed Osiris down to the smallest detail, creating the first perfect couple.

Osiris and Isis also had a brother called Seth. Where Osiris was kind and wise, Seth was unruly and envious. He hated Osiris so much that he actually murdered him for the throne of Egypt.

Nephthys, their sister (and Seth's partner), attempted to stop the murder, but she did not manage to do it.

And so, Seth's evil plan was taken to an end. However, Osiris was resurrected by Isis through her magic—and he impregnated her with Horus. Later on, Horus grew to avenge his father and take back the throne of Egypt while Osiris retired to the Otherworld to rule over the deceased souls. By doing this, he established the cycle of life and resurrection that fueled so many of the actions Egyptians took on a day to day basis (including how they were buried).

Many other gods and goddesses entered the realm of Egyptian Mythology. But Ra, Osiris, and Isis remained the staple characters of a story that lasted for as long as Ancient Egypt survived. These myths are not just fantasy stories for us today: they are testimonies of a very advanced civilization that treasured not only war and technology, but also storytelling, beauty, and philosophy, mirroring, perhaps, changes in both society and ways of thinking.

The Story of Ra

Ra created the world and, because humans were dear to him, he also wanted to show them how to live better. So he took the shape of a human and lived among them as a pharaoh.

But at some point, the world stopped liking him, and humans rebelled against the sun god. Upon seeing this, Ra got (obviously) upset, and so he decided to exterminate the world. He asked his tear-giving eye for help, and she became a lioness who started to slaughter mankind.

The carnage brought Ra to tears, and he stopped it for the sake of all the children that were dying. However, he refused to stay among humans anymore and moved to the Otherworld.

That is when the 12-hour day was created (as Ra traveled for 12 hours from East to West, as the sun god, illuminating everything that came his way). When he reached the Western world, he went into darkness and created nighttime as he sailed to the Underworld. In his journey, he destroyed the enemies of creation and regenerated himself as a union with Osiris.

When Ra (as his new self) re-appeared in the Eastern skies, he did it as a falcon that came to be known as Horus. Throughout his adventures, Ra took other forms as well, such as the form of a scarab. Each of his forms came with a special name that had a lot of meaning attached to it. For instance, his falcon form was associated with the name "Hor-akhty" (which means "the one who is high up"). Furthermore, his scarab form was called "Kheper" (the one who comes into being).

At sunrise, Ra showed himself as the falcon. By midday, he had returned as the god Ra in the shape of a sun disk. At the end of the day, he transformed himself into Atum (an old man who had already completed his life cycle and was on the verge of disappearing to regenerate for another day).

Ra was the ultimate god of the Egyptians. From the Old Kingdom onwards (when kings were appointed as sons of Ra), Ra ruled supreme over the banks of the Nile (until the end of the Empire). There were times in history when Ra was forcefully made to be the *only* god (such as during the reign of Akhenaton). And there were times when Ra collided with other gods (such as Amon-Ra and Sobek-Ra, for example).

But through the thick and thin, through the ups and downs, and through the growth and retreat of the Egyptian glory, the sun god guarded his people into the light again, and again.

Ra finally saw his demise when Romans finally conquered Egypt, and the banks of the Nile changed forever.

Ra left behind songs so marvelous they are echoed even in the main monotheistic religions. He also left behind a legacy that keeps him alive in everything ranging from Ancient Egyptian artifacts to Hollywood movies.

The sun god is a true symbol of Ancient Egypt and its tumultuous history, a mythological mirror of the struggles, passions, successes, and failures of the people who built their lives around the River Nile. A metaphor for the birth of the sun and the passing of days and nights themselves, the Sun God Ra, came to be a story intrinsic to the very blood and air of Ancient Egyptians (Haikal, n.d.).

Isis and Osiris

Isis and Osiris might be one of the first love stories ever recorded—and not just any kind of love story, but a tragic one about commitment, loyalty, and fierce strength.

There are several versions of how Osiris came to be murdered, slaughtered, and shattered into pieces by his brother, Seth. One of the versions says he committed adultery with his sister or sister in law, Nephthys. Another one says he kicked Seth. Either way, it seems that Osiris did something to terribly upset Seth in all versions, which led to the scenario where Isis found herself childless and mourning for her husband/ brother.

That did not last for long, though. Together with her sister (and Seth's wife), Nephthys, Isis managed to find all the pieces of Osiris and bring them back together with the help of two other gods (Anubis and Toth, both gods of death). She then wrapped all the pieces of Osiris like a mummy, transformed into a kite, flew around him, drew his seed, and became pregnant. This led her to give birth to Horus (Hansen, 2020).

In other versions of the story of Isis and Osiris, Osiris was first caged in a wooden box and thrown in the Nile. Isis searched for her husband far and wide, brought him back home, only to outrage Seth even more (which caused him to hack his brother into pieces). From here on, though, the story goes the same as the one mentioned above.

In both scenarios, Osiris ended up neither alive nor dead. Unable to find a place in the world anymore, Osiris retreated to the Land of the Dead and became their king and judge. Before he left, though, he reassured Isis that she would bear a son, Horus, who would win over Seth and become the King of Egypt, and this did happen.

Before Horus came of age, however, Isis hid with him on the banks of the Nile River, all the while protecting him from harm. Some accounts speak about spells she threw over Horus to protect him from snakes and scorpions—spells that were also used by human mothers to protect their own real children from the very same real dangers.

Isis is one of the most interesting images in the history of Egyptian Mythology. She is unique because she was not revered too much before the dynastic age. However, she soon became one of the most beloved and well-known gods of Egypt. Even more, she remained extremely popular long after Ancient Egypt's Empire fell. Even today, she is worshipped by pagans, and many women in Egypt still referred to her as a healer and magician up to the 14th century C.E. (long after Islam became the majority religion in Egypt).

Isis played a crucial role in the birth and protection of a young Horus and the buril rituall that was so important for Egyptians. A mother, healer, and an essential element in the resurrection of the dead in the afterlife, Isis became central to the entire culture, civilization, and religion of Ancient Egypt (and well beyond, since, at some point, even Romans worshipped her).

It is generally believed that Egyptians thought that all people who die become like Osiris (and this is why they are buried in chests and wrapped around like mummies). In the perspective of Ancient Egyptians, all humans were to go to the afterlife and be born again, just like Osiris.

The story of Isis and Osiris is a story of resilience and pure love. Although they did end up apart (with Osiris in the Land of the Dead and Isis above), their lives on Earth were associated with a flourishing Egypt precisely because both of them contributed to the well-being of the Egyptians. Even more, their story is the very reason that gave Egyptians hope in the afterlife, showing that love (and, well, maybe a little bit of magic) can do *anything* (Mark, 2016).

Horus and Seth

In most modern representations, Seth is seen as the representation of the ultimate evil. A god of chaos, war, and storms, he is, indeed, associated with bad things that happened to humans.

But our understanding of Seth might be skewed a little by how Christians, Muslims, and Jews see Lucifer himself as the representation of evil. In reality, Egyptians might have had a more balanced view of Seth and his role in the universe.

For much of his "life" as an Egyptian God, Seth was actually seen as a benevolent super-being. In the beginning, he was one of the first gods (among the first five, actually, all of which were brothers and sisters and had the same father and mother—the sky and the earth) (Mark, 2016).

In some stories, he is even shown to help the Sun God Ra when his journey from night to day when the serpent Apophis tried to prevent this from happening. In doing this, Seth helped daylight come to the world again.

In many other accounts, he is associated with love spells on amulets or even the dead's main care provider in the afterlife. All these stories show Seth was not always the "bad guy" of Ancient Egyptian mythology.

However, his status changed when he became the first murderer, killing his brother Osiris. As mentioned in the previous story, Osiris was brought back to life by Isis (with the help of Nephthys, who was also Seth's wife and all of their sister).

Upon bringing Osiris back to life, Isis became impregnated with Horus, who was foretold to be the one to defeat Seth and take back the throne of Egypt. This prediction did become real, but there are several accounts on *how* exactly it did.

In some of them, Horus grows up and challenges Seth in battle, defeating him and taking the throne from him, finally freeing Egyptians from his uncle's chaotic rule.

In others, however, the battle between Horus and Seth is a little more complicated. It involves not only the two of them but also the nine major gods and the intervention of Isis, Horus' mother.

The story between Horus and Seth became somewhat clearer when *The Contendings of Horus and Seth* came to light. In this papyrus, Horus and Seth fight for the throne of Egypt by overcoming several obstacles. Their entire fight is "juried" by the nine main gods of Egypt (including the Sun God Ra), and unanimity must be attained through their votes for one of the contenders to be elected as the King of Egypt.

Although most of the gods are convinced that Horus is entitled to the throne, the sun god is not that certain of this. Although Seth was chaotic, he believed that he had already proven himself a worthy leader (whereas Horus was still very young and had lived a sheltered life).

To convince him of Horus' cause, Isis transforms herself into an ordinary woman and shows herself in Seth's path. She cries and tells her the story of how her husband's lands were usurped by his brother and how her son cannot get back what is rightfully his. Upon hearing this story and seeing the woman's pain, Seth is touched and vows to find the usurper and punish him himself. When Seth says this, Isis shows herself with her true face, revealing the witnessing gods as well. This is when Ra is convinced Horus should take the throne of Egypt. In this version. Seth ends up driven out into the desert.

Another version of *The Contendings of Horus and Seth* shows that unable to reach an agreement, the gods ask the goddess Neith to preside over the debate. She was seen as a very wise goddess and it is believed that she had taken the role of intermediary between gods before the battle of Horus and Seth. She finds a middle ground solution for the issue of who should reign over Egypt. More specifically, she suggests that Horus should take the throne of Egypt, and Seth should be given the desert lands and the foreign lands (alongside the promise to get Anat and Astarte, two foreign goddesses, as his consorts).

What is extremely interesting about this recount of the story is that Neith was a goddess mostly worshipped in the Predynastic period. Thus, her role as a mediator and wise woman was transferred to Isis when she became the main womanly figure of Egyptian mythology.

In all versions of the story, however, Horus sets himself as the rightful ruler of Egypt. Perhaps oddly enough for modern sensitivities, he takes Isis as his ruling consort and reigns over Egypt for many years, just as his father had before him.

What is absolutely fascinating is that, although Seth did lose the throne of Egypt, he continued to be considered one of the most important Egyptian Kings. In fact, he was so essential to the existence of Egyptian mythology that Peribsen, one of the Kings in the Second Dynasty, chose Seth as his patron god.

This is intriguing because, by that time, Horus was the god of choice for all Kings. It made sense: Horus ruled over Egypt on Earth, and thus, the pharaoh was his human representative (one to become Osiris in death, of course).

It is quite interesting then to ask ourselves why exactly did Peribsen choose to be identified with Seth. Some Egyptologists believe this is related to the fact that many Kings before him chose to be associated with Ra. Most times, Ra was tightly connected to Horus, so it also made sense for pharaohs to make this choice. However, since Seth had protected Ra in his fight with Apophis, Ra was frequently connected to Seth as well, so it is this line of thought that might have made Peribsen choose Seth as his patron God.

Other egyptologists believe that Perbisen came from Upper Egypt and chose to be associated with Seth simply because Horus was more connected to Lower Egypt. This is, one of the theories that are closest to reality, as it seems like a more logical conclusion than departing from Horus as a patron god just for "the sake of it" (which is how the previously mentioned theory appears to be).

However, in all cases, Seth is not seen as the all-evil god we'd probably be tempted to portray through our modern views. He was a god (a flawed one, at that), and he continued to play a very important role for Egyptians until the fall of the Empire.

The Story of Anubis

Although a preeminent figure in Ancient Egypt, Anubis is not present in many of the stories that make up the realm of Egyptian mythology. Even more than that, Anubis is a very interesting figure because his role changed quite a lot over the course of history (but he always remained at the center of interest among all other Egyptian gods) (Mark, 2016).

Anubis is believed to be one of the oldest Ancient Egyptian gods. He is frequently represented as a black dog or as a hybrid between a jackal and a dog. His representation as a *black* dog or jackal has nothing to do with the colors of these animals though. In fact, Egyptians depicted Anubis as black for two main reasons.

The first one is because they associated black with the color of decay (and throughout his entire journey among the Egyptian gods, Anubis was always associated with the dead, one way or another).

The second reason Anubis is depicted as black is related to the banks of the River Nile. Black and fertile, this soil was representative of decay and rebirth, which made a lot of sense, especially when Anubis was associated with the afterlife.

The birth of Anubis is debated, depending on what period of Egyptian history you look at. Before the Middle Kingdom (which is when Osiris grew in popularity), Anubis was believed to be the son of the Sun God Ra and Hesat.

After Osiris took the central role in the Land of the Dead, Anubis began to be associated with his son (where Nephthys, the wife and sister of Seth was his mother). In this storyline, Nephthys herself is seen as a friend of the dead (and somewhat of a partner in the ruling of the Land of the Dead, together with Osiris). Even more, in stories where Osiris is already popularly seen as the King of the Dead, Anubis helps to embalm his body when Isis and Nephthys bring him back to life.

Anubis' role does not become unimportant when Osiris rises as the main ruler of the afterlife. On the contrary, Anubis, Osiris, and sometimes other gods (such as Toth, another god associated with the afterlife) all play a part in weighing the soul of each dead person that reaches the Hall of Truth.

Before Osiris rose as the god of the afterlife (after his death and resurrection), Anubis was the one in charge of the lost souls. He went by many names, one of which was "The First of the Westerners" (not because he came from the West, but because Egyptians believed the souls of the dead were always heading West, where the sun sets).

After Osiris became popular, Anubis continued to be associated with the dead, but more as a secondary god of the afterlife than as the main protector of the souls that passed away.

You might find it quite interesting that Anubis battled Seth as well. When Isis brought back the pieces that made up Osiris' body, Seth sought, by all means, to destroy him again.

In one story, the body of Osiris was kept in the place of embalming during this process. Seth noticed that Anubis leaves the place every night and transformed into Anubis to trick the guards and steal Osiris' body.

Anubis discovered the theft and went to search for Seth. Seth turned into a bull toward him off, but Anubis defeated, captured, and imprisoned him in Saka. Seth escaped his imprisonment and went back to his plan of stealing and destroying Osiris' body. This time, he turned into a big cat, but Anubis caught him again and branded him with hot irons (which is how Egyptians explained the birth of leopards, actually).

Even after doing this, Seth did not give up on his plan. He turned himself into Anubis and got caught again. In this instance, he was sentenced to become Osiris' throne for the rest of eternity.

It seems that one of Seth's main redemptive qualities was never giving up because even after being sentenced to be a throne for eternity, he still went on with his plan. This time, it was his last attempt, though, because Anubis caught him, flayed his skin, and set his body on fire. He also went on to slay Seth's entire army with a single slash of his sword. Egyptians believed the place where Seth's army was killed was red with their blood. More modern science has proven that it was just a mineral in the soil that made it look reddish, of course—but it is still extremely interesting to see how Ancient Egyptians found mythical explanations for the natural phenomenon they noticed.

Another story features Anubis outside of the Osiris myth, showing that he existed both as Osiris' son (and his precursor in the Land of the Dead in some depictions), and as a stand-alone god.

In this myth, Bata, Anubis' brother, was working on his farm one day when he stumbled upon Anubis' wife. She invited him into her bed, but Bata turned down her offer, saying that she has been like a mother to him and that what she is proposing was an abomination. You see, Ancient Egyptians did not have a very clear stance of incest and adultery, as this myth shows when compared to other, perhaps more fundamental stories of their mythology (such as Isis, who was a sister and a wife to Osiris, and later on a consort to their own son).

Going back to Bata and Anubis' story, it seems that Anubis' wife felt quite hurt by Bata's refusal. When Anubis came home, she pretended she had been propositioned by Bata, then beaten when she refused.

Naturally, Anubis was enraged by her story and wanted to kill his brother. However, divine intervention prevented him from doing this, and, in the end, he listened to Bata's side of the story. To prove he was sincere, Bata cut off his penis and threw it into the River. Then, he promised to move to the Valley of the Cedars, where he promised to connect his heart with the top of a cedar (and if the cedar was cut down, he would die)

Bata lived there alone for quite some time until Ra-Herakhty ordered Khnum to create a wife for Bata out of his pottery wheel. Both Bata and his wife lived happily, but not "forever after," because soon, the Seven Hathors came and foretold that Bata's wife would have an unhappy end.

Bata grew very worried about this prophecy and told his wife to take very good care of herself (along with the fact that cutting the cedar tree would lead to his death). He tried to protect her as much as he could, but one day, the sea tried to take Bata's wife from him. She managed to flee, but the sea took away a lock of her hair, which ended up in the hands of the King of Egypt.

Enchanted by the aroma of this strand of hair, the King of Egypt ordered for the owner of the hair to be found.

Eventually, the king found her, and she told him about the cedar tree and her husband's heart. The king then had the tree cut down, which led Bata to die, as he prophesied. As Bata also prophesied, Anubis came to look for him and was deeply saddened to find that the cedar tree had been cut off.

He took both Bata's body to bring back home for burial and a berry from the tree. When he got back home, he placed the tree in a cup of water. The seed did not sprout normally, though, as it revealed Bata himself. The body of Bata drank the seed and came back to life and learned that the king had married his ex-wife.

To help Bata avenge the injustice, Anubis gave the king a bull as a gift (but what the king did not know was that the bull was actually Bata). Anubis's brother then went through a series of transformations and ended up as a splinter in the Queen's mouth, which impregnated her, which gave birth to a baby boy (who was also Bata, I know this is getting quite complicated). This also meant that Bata (his former husband) became her son (which brings us back to incest).

The king died, and Bata (as the Queen's son) took power. When this happened, he testified against his wife and mother and disgraced her. Then, he appointed Anubis as his crown prince and, when Bata died, he succeeded him as king (Meehan, n.d.).

As it can be easily noticed, Anubis had quite the journey as an Egyptian God, and many stories will portray him differently (or at least in different settings). If one thing is for certain, though, it is that Anubis played an essential role for Egyptians (which is why he remains one of the most easily noticeable figures in all of the hieroglyphs and Ancient Egyptian paintings we have found to the date).

The Book of Thoth

For a people who placed such massive importance on death, it should come as no surprise that they had several representations of gods that dealt in the realm of the souls.

Thoth is one of them (and quite a central figure in Ancient Egyptian mythology as well). However, unlike Anubis, Osiris, Nephthys, and others, Thoth's association is not directly linked to death itself, but to the wider concept of wisdom (which includes helping judge the dead souls in the Hall of Truth as well).

Greeks associated Thoth with Hermes (and even believed he is a different, mightier incarnation of their own God). They did this because Thoth was frequently believed to be the god of wisdom, writing, magic, and the moon (Mark, 2016).

One of the most interesting appearances Thoth makes in Egyptian Mythology is during the battle between Seth and Horus. In some stories, he is actually born from the two of them when, during a battle, Seth accidentally swallows Horus' semen. Thus, Thoth is born and becomes one of the main mediators between the two during their battle.

This is quite symbolic of the concept of balance (ma'at), which was very important for Ancient Egyptians. Born between chaos and order (Seth and Horus), Thoth becomes the wisest path to success.

In other stories, Thoth is born from Ra's lips at the beginning of creation, which is also quite symbolic. If the sun god gave birth to a son from his own lips, and this son guarded over writing and wisdom, then it means that both of these were essentially great in the eyes of Ra.

The Book of Thoth is a rather mysterious collection of texts that have been supposedly attributed to the god Thoth. Although no real evidence has been brought forward to support the idea that this book actually exists, modern fiction has placed it at the center of plenty of Ancient Egyptian-themed books and movies.

The Book of Thoth is not a mere supposition, as it seems to appear in a couple of other stories, references as a book in those stories (which makes this entire deal seem quite "meta", right?).

Interestingly enough, the Book of Thoth is talked about in a story whose main moral is "humans are not supposed to know the secrets of the gods." In this story (called Setne I), the Book of Thoth wrote his Book and included in it two very powerful spells: one to help humans understand the speech of animals and help them see the actual presence of the gods.

The book was hidden at the bottom of the Nile River in a box guarded by serpents. The Book of Thoth stayed there until Neferkaptah, an Egyptian Prince, fought the serpents and retrieved the book. Thoth was enraged with this theft and cursed Neferkaptah by killing his wife and son. Soon after, prince Neferkaptah committed suicide and was buried with the Book of Thoth.

Many generations later, Setne Khamwas finds the book by opening Neferkaptah's tomb. Although the ghost of the prince fights it, Setne steals the book. He then meets a beautiful woman who convinces him to kill his children and humiliate himself in front of the pharaoh. Setne then discovers that this had all been an illusion created by Neferkaptah's ghost, so, fearing that something even worse would happen, he returns the book to the tomb and seals it (Lichteim, 2006).

There is no clear evidence of the actual existence of such a book, although many speculations have been made. To date, the Book of Thoth remains one of the most awe-inspiring mysteries of Ancient Egypt.

The Princess of Bekhten

The story of the Princess of Bekhten was created to add a mythical layer to how the riches of the Great Temple of Khosu in Thebes came to be. Khosu, the central god of this story, was also considered to be a different form of Thoth (precisely because both are lunar gods that deal in magic).

It is worth noting that the story of the Princess of Bekhten was recorded much later than the building of the Great Temple in Thebes (which was actually erected during Ramses III).

According to the story, the King of Egypt (assumed to be Ramses II himself) was in the country of Nehern, collecting his annual tribute. Most princes of the country brought him various riches, such as gold, turquoise, and lapis-lazuli. However, the prince of Bekhten brought him his own daughter.

Smitten with her amazing beauty, the king accepted the prince's tribute and took the girl back home to make her the chief royal consort (under the name of Ra-neferu, meaning "the beauty of Ra").

The two lived very happily until one day, the prince of Bekhten sent an envoy to the king and asked him to send a healer for the Queen's younger sister, who was incredibly ill. The king chose Tehuti-em-beb (a scribe) to send back to Bekhten to help his sister in law.

Upon getting there, Tehuti-em-beb realized that he could not help the princess because an evil spirit had possessed her. So, he returned back to Egypt.

Not much later on, the prince of Bekhten sent word to the king again, asking even more fervently for his help. Upon hearing that his scribe had not succeeded, the king went into the temple of Khonsu and asked the god himself to go and heal the princess of Bekhten. Khonsu set off on a journey to Bekhten, which took no less than 17 months.

Khonsu did manage to instantly heal the princess and make the demon leave her body. he demon submitted to the god's power and promised to go back to his lands if Khonsu were to throw a dinner together with him and the prince of Bekhten, which he did, and they were all happy.

The story shows that Khonsu stayed in Bekhten for three years, as the prince asked him to linger on more (especially since he had witnessed the real powers of the God). After a while, though, Khonsu returned back home to Egypt, from whence he was summoned back to Bekhten again to receive gifts of gratitude from the prince.

It is said that Khonsu did return to receive his gifts and then brought them home to Thebes to the temple of Khonsu Nefer-hetep.

Khonsu went on to be a highly regarded god for Ancient Egyptian priests and magicians who relied on the god's power to help them heal, perform miracles, and vanquish the demons (Egyptian Myths, n.d.).

The Prince and the Sphinx

The story of the Prince and the Sphinx is at least partly true (as we have proof of it). Even more than that, it is incredibly revealing over just what a *long time* Egypt reigned supreme in its area.

Thutmose was the son of King Amenhotep, and while he was still a prince, it is believed that his (many) brothers constantly belittled him in front of their father. You see, Thutmose was a bit of a rebel himself. He didn't like grand proceedings and events and preferred running to the edge of the desert to hunt or spend time alone. Even so, and despite all his brothers' efforts, he was still his father's favorite.

Thutmose's brothers tried everything to discredit him, from making people believe he was too extravagant to actually attempting to murder him (on not one, but two occasions!).

Thutmose remained the same, though. He frequently ran away as quickly as he could whenever he had an obligation to attend special events and preferred to spend his time training himself in different sports rather than participate in the official proceedings and festivals.

It is said that, once, while he was at the Festival of Ra in Memphis, Thutmose snuck away to hunt at the edge of the desert. The story shows him racing away in his own chariot, well past the step pyramid of Djoser and close to the Great Pyramids. He and the two people he brought along with him settled down for a bit, as it was too hot for hunting by that time of the day.

Restless and wanting to pray to the god Harmachis, Thutmose left his people behind and drove off into the desert. There, he stumbled upon a structure that looked like the head and neck of a pharaoh god sculpted in stone but buried in the sand.

Judging by the surprise Thutmose had, seeing what we now know as the Sphinx, it is easy to see that a long time had passed since Khafra's reign (history tells us there is a 1,200-year gap between Thutmose and Khafra, to be more specific). It is also clear that even for Egyptians, some of the structures that we marvel at today were still unknown and rather mysterious.

As he was looking at the Sphinx, Thutmose saw it come to life, and it told him that he should be the chosen one to rule over Egypt. The image of the Great Sphinx, showing himself as Harmachis touched Thutmose deeply. As such, he vowed that, when he will become the next pharaoh, he will uncover the Sphinx and make sure everyone sees it. Even more, he also vowed to build a shrine for Harmachis right on the basis of the Sphinx.

More than 3,000 years after Thutmose's rise to the kingdom, an early archeologist uncovered the Sphinx, buried under sand one more time. Between the feet of this magnificent structure, he also found a 14-feet high tablet that spoke of Thutmose's story and his encounter with the Sphinx (Egyptian Myths, n.d.)

We might not know if the Sphinx actually came to life, but we do know even for an Ancient Egyptian, this structure was truly awe-inspiring and magical, just as we "sense" it today as well.

Isis and the Seven Scorpions

After the murder of Osiris, Isis was forced into hiding, but Seth found her and locked her up in a spinning mill. There, she was sentenced to spin Osiris' burial linen. However, Thoth feared that she would be in danger if Seth found out she was pregnant, so he came to rescue her. To do that, he asked for the help of seven scorpions (called Tefen, Masetetef, Petet, Tjetet, Matet, Mesetet, and Befen) (Ancient Egypt Online, n.d.).

Isis escaped Seth's imprisonment, protected under the oath of the seven scorpions. To make sure she was safe, she took the form of an old beggar and wandered, looking for shelter. At some point, she asked a rich lady for help, but seeing her as a beggar, she was very rude to Isis and did not aid her in any way.

After a while, Isis reached a fisherman's daughter who warmly offered her shelter and food. The seven scorpions did not forget about the rich lady's rudeness, though, so they attacked her baby.

Desperate, the rich lady ran into town, looking for help, but nobody could do anything for her. Hearing the baby's cries, though, Isis felt pity and ordered the poison to leave the child's body. Realizing that she had banished the goddess herself from her house, the rich lady felt a lot of remorse and gave her entire fortune to the fisherman's daughter.

This basic story behind this myth is a recurrent one throughout the entirety of ancient civilization. For example, just like Egyptians, Greeks believed they are indebted to offering shelter to any beggar and any person that comes to their door—precisely because they never knew when a god or goddess could appear in disguise.

These are, of course, just a few of the many, many stories that compiled what we now know as the "Egyptian mythology." As you can see from these stories, the gods and goddesses of Ancient Egypt were not only super-natural but also possessed very *human* traits.

They were neither black nor white. They got angry and resented their mistakes. They fell in love and fell in wrath. They fought each other and supported each other. They loved and hated with passion (so much so that they were sometimes ready to murder or bring their loved ones back from death).

Throughout their histories, though, these gods were very much *alive*. The meaning of their attributions and myths changed in time and adapted to new societies, new technology, and even new gods.

Nothing was ever static under the skies and in the afterlife of Ancient Egypt. And that makes it one of the most complex and interesting mythologies to study today.

In the next chapter, I will attempt to make quick descriptions of some of Egypt's most important gods . Of course, you will already be familiar with some of them (as we have discussed them in this chapter as well). But you will most definitely have the opportunity to see them in new lights, with new faces, and, perhaps, in different contexts than they were presented in this chapter.

Let's roll!

Chapter 5: Egyptian Gods and Goddesses

It is believed the Egyptian pantheon included no less than 2,000 names (Mark, 2016).

That might sound like a shocking and perhaps unrealistic number, but do keep in mind that Egyptian mythology was forever-changing, forever-adapting, forever-shifting its facets and names, forever running with the times, economy, society, and pharaohs that ruled over the country.

By comparison, Greek mythology had twelve main gods (the Olympians) and several hundreds of other smaller gods or mythical figures that were more or less deified (including demi-gods).

And to compare Egyptians to an even larger number, it is estimated that Hinduism has more than *33 million* gods (Mark, 2016). Of course, all of these gods have very niche attributions, so you would much rather associate this with the structure of a corporation rather than a pantheon in the way most modern people imagine it.

Leaving aside the number, it might sound maybe even more shocking to learn that the vast majority of these gods had at least a small connection to the idea of death. One way or another, everything in Egypt revolved around two pillars: death and the Nile.

No matter how you look at it, Egyptian mythology is intricate and twisted, so I cannot even aim to try and encompass *all* the gods in just one chapter of one book. As is the case with all the myths and the real-life stories and mysteries of Ancient Egypt, it would take entire libraries to do that.

Instead, what I would like to do is walk you through some of the most important gods of Egypt and help you understand their multifaceted destinies, names, and personalities.

So, without further ado, let's dive right into this and try to untangle (at least a little) the otherwise fascinating Egyptian pantheon.

Ra, The Sun God

Without a doubt, Ra is one of the single most crucial gods in the entire Egyptian pantheon. A very old god, Ra appears to have been the result of a fusion between multiple Sun-cults. While it is not exactly known what those cults were like, the assumption is made based on the fact that Egyptians emphasized the power of the sun as a creator long before Ra came into the picture.

However, what is clear is that the sun god was seen as the one who controlled the day and night. Every 24 hours, he traveled on a boat to bring the light back to Egypt. In his journey, he was sometimes accompanied by Horus, Thoth, Ma'At, and, in some depictions, by Anubis, and he always fought the serpent Apophis (the representative of the night).

Because Egyptians treasured Ra so much, his cult was frequently merged with other cults and deities. As such, several "versions" or facets of Ra were born, including the following:

Ra-Tem

The temple at Heliopolis was built to worship the sun god. However, Ra had not always been the main god of the sun in Atum, where the temple was erected. Thus, when Ra "came" there, he was merged with the local god Temu (also a solar god). As such, Ra became Ra-Tem here.

At some point in Egyptian history, the powers of Ra started to diminish, but the Heliopolis temple was rebuilt as a dedication to Ra and two of his forms (one as Horus, and the other one as Temu) (Spence, 1990).

Amun-Ra

The story of how Amun and Ra came to be merged is quite complex. On the one hand, Amun was considered to be an old god in charge with the sun and the air. As a creation of Amunet, Amun's name alluded to something that cannot be seen.

Some believe that Amun-Ra represented the night journey of Ra around Earth. However, it is more likely that the fusion between Ra and Amun was more related to wind rather than Ra's solar journey (Mark, 2016; Spence, 1990).

Ra-Horakhty

In an age when Horus was already an important deity, some stories point out the existence of a so-called "Ra-Horakhty," who was an instance of both Horus and Ra dealing with the sunrise. In this instance, Ra is seen as a god of rebirth and hope, precisely because sunrise always elicits those feelings in humans.

Khepera

Before he left Earth on his journey to bring daytime to Egypt, Ra also left behind a human form, known as Khepera (commonly represented as a scarab rolling in the morning sun). This is the deity associated with creation and is also believed to be the true father of the "Nine Gods" known as The Ennead.

Shu

As one of the very first gods to be born out of Atum-Ra, Shu is the brother and spouse of Tefnut. He is the god of air, so he is considered to be a calming, pacifying presence. However, in some stories, he and Tefnut (the goddess of moisture and rain) are said to have fought, which led to huge storms in Egypt. Again, as you can see, Egyptians (and pretty much all other polytheistic societies) used gods to explain natural phenomena in magical ways.

Tefnut

Sister and wife of Shu, Tefnut is, as mentioned above, the goddess of rain, moisture, and dew. Most of the stories depicting her creation involve some sort of body fluid (which, together with her name that meant "That Water," makes quite a lot of sense given that she was the one to control fluids on Earth). Together with her twin brother, Shu, Tefnut will give to Nut and Geb, who, in their turn, will give birth to the other gods.

Nut

She is one of the Nine Ra created in his instance as Amun-Ra, on the island we mentioned at the beginning of the book. Seen as the goddess of the sky and cosmos, Nut played a big part in creating the other gods, as she is the mother of Osiris, Isis, Seth, and Nephthys. It is believed that Ra caught Nut and Geb in the act of love when he decided to separate them, thus giving birth to the duality between the sky and the earth (and also that between night and day, good and evil). Before they were separated, however, Nut gave birth to the aforementioned gods.

Geb

Nut's brother and spouse and son of Shu and Tefnut, Geb is the god of Earth. He is sometimes seen as a healer and a god of vegetation. Many times he is associated with the goddess of harvest. Other times, however, Geb is also feared because he is believed to be the father of all snakes (which were, as you might guess, is associated with the earth).

Osiris

Also a figure central to the Egyptian pantheon, Osiris' story is one that has survived to the date. If pop culture doesn't speak that much about his parents and grandparents, it sure does include him in a lot of stories.

Osiris is an archetypal representation of mortality and rebirth in all its forms: day and night, agricultural cycles, the afterlife, fertility, and so on. Different stories depict him in different ways, but he always maintains this duality between life and death, passing away and being born again.

Isis

A figure of femininity, motherhood, healing, and magic, Isis is perhaps one of the longest-standing gods of Egypt. As I was saying in the previous chapter, the cult of Isis continued to survive long after Egyptians lost interest in Osiris—and to date, she is still seen as a patron of womanhood everywhere.

Seth

As also explained in the previous chapter, Seth has been long seen as the bad guy. Before we even attempt to resemble him with Lucifer from the Abrahamic tradition, though, it is important to remember that the concept of balance (between, well, *everything*) was absolutely paramount for Ancient Egyptians.

In other words, there would be no good without the bad—and as such, Seth plays an essential role in bringing the good into the world. Chaotic and sometimes seen as a god of war, Seth is nothing but a player in the great cosmic balance, and for this reason, he was still worshipped and respected.

Nephthys

The wife of Seth and potentially mistress of Osiris, and the sister of Seth, Isis, and Osiris at the same time, Nephthys is one of the less popular Egyptian gods these days. It is not clear why exactly she went into a pseudo-obscurity in time, but what is definitely known is that she was not at all unknown during the times of Ancient Egypt.

Nephthys, like Anubis, and also like her siblings, is frequently associated with death. In fact, she is seen as a protector of mummies, as a goddess of mourning, the night (as a concept and a reality), and also a guardian of childbirth. Perhaps oddly enough, she is also associated with beer.

Horus

The latest comer into the Ennead, Horus is a figure so typical and so essential to Egyptian mythology that we cannot really imagine it without him. As the god of the sky and a protector of kingship, Horus is present throughout the entire life of the Egyptian Empire. Sometimes, he even takes his father's role (as the Golden Horus), and other times he *is* Osiris himself, in his earthly form.

The conflict between Horus and Seth remains one of the first and most fascinating fights between good and evil, rightful heir and usurper, day and night—a conflict which, as explained before, is essential to how Egyptians viewed life (and death).

Anubis

Mostly considered to be a secondary deity (in the sense that he was not part of the original Nine Gods), Anubis is incredibly popular even today. Everyone has at least seen one representation of Anubis as a black dog or Chakal. Just like his mother, he is associated with mummification and the afterlife, and he is commonly seen as a protector of the lost souls and the helpless. It is generally believed that Anubis existed under a different name (Wepwawet) before the First Dynasty as well. So, even if he is a latecomer in the Origin Story of the Egyptian gods, he is still considered to be one of the oldest deities in Egypt.

Thoth

Thoth is a very interesting god for many reasons. He protects writing, wisdom, magic, and healing, but unlike most other gods, he was not born out of a father and a mother, but from the fight between Horus and Seth.

That is actually very meaningful and symbolic of how Egyptians saw true wisdom: as the balance between good and evil and chaos and order. Thoth is the embodiment of this kind of wisdom, and stories depicting him almost always associate him with negotiation, diplomacy, and magical healing.

Ma'At

Since we have been mentioning the Ancient Egyptian concept of balance quite a lot, it is more than worth including Ma'At here as well. In the Ancient Egyptian language, "Ma'at" was used both as a proper noun (to represent the goddess) and as a common noun (to describe the concept of balance we have already discussed).

As a goddess, Ma'At represented truth, balance, harmony, and justice and was frequently represented either wearing an ostrich feather or simply as a white ostrich feather. It is also important to know that although the first mentions of her date back to the Old Kingdom, it is quite likely that she had been present in Egypt long before that.

Apep/Apophis

If you ever have to name a bad guy in all of the Egyptian mythology, name Apophis. It is generally believed that Apophis always existed, long before the Sun God Ra brought order into the world. In fact, one of the reasons Apophis was so angry with Ra was because he was a threat to the singularity of chaos and darkness he was so comfortable living (and thriving in).

As mentioned before, Apophis fought Ra when he tried to bring sunlight back every day as he traveled around Earth. However, he was always defeated (and this is why he is sometimes represented as beaten).

Alas, you would think that, since Apophis represented darkness, oblivion, and forgetting one's identity, Egyptians did not include him much in their rituals. However, they did—and most of these rituals revolved around, you guessed it, *balance*.

Bastet

It is a well-known fact that Egyptians really liked their cats. What most people might not know, though, is that they even had a cat goddess: Bastet. Although she was not the first cat goddess in the history of Egypt, Bastet remains one of the most popular ones.

Overall, she was seen as the goddess of home, protector of childbirth, and the secrets of women, but sometimes she is also associated with the god of perfume and nice smells. Even more, on many occasions, she is represented as a fierce lioness and even helped Ra fight Apophis during their great battle.

Sekhmet

Sekhmet is usually represented as a lioness, considering she is one of the most important feminine characters of Egyptian Mythology. She is seen as a goddess of both destruction and healing. However, in time, her attributions shifted towards the military and vengeance. She is believed to bring destruction (including through the winds of the desert or the plague). Also, she is the one Ra sends to slaughter mankind when he becomes angry with them.

Hathor

Hathor is a very powerful goddess of Ancient Egypt as well. She has a dual nature because, on the one hand, she is one and the same with Sekhmet, but after slaughtering mankind, Ra tricks her into drinking reddened beer. When she wakes up, she is benevolent, and she becomes the goddess of music and drunkenness. In time, her meaning shifts, and she becomes the Mother Goddess, a very feminine and motherly figure for Egyptians.

Ptah

This god is dated from the First Dynasty, but it is generally believed that he was present in the lives of Egyptians long before the dynasties. Sometimes seen as a god of agriculture and fertility and other times is seen as the creator of the world itself, Ptah remained a preeminent figure in Egyptian mythology even long after Ra became the father of all creation.

Small Deities

Aside from the nine major gods and all the others presented in this list, Egyptians also had a long list of smaller deities. Most of the times, their attributions were very niche, such as:

- Min, the god of Virility
- Baal, the god of Storm ("borrowed" from Canaan and worshipped by Egyptians during the First Kingdom)
- Setem, a deity of healing
- Sopd, the god of the Eastern Delta
- Anket, a goddess of fertility and a representation of the Nile cataract at Aswan
- Sia, the deified personification of perception

As mentioned at the beginning of this chapter, more than 2,000 deities are recorded in the Egyptian pantheon. While not all of them pertain to Egyptians per se (as they were sometimes influenced by their neighboring countries and Greeks and Romans), they were all worshipped at one point or another.

Throughout their entire history, Ancient Egyptian deities lived and died for one purpose: to ensure the balance in the world of human Egyptians. They fought, they committed adultery and incest, the murdered, and then they brought back to life—because while life and death were entirely in their hands, they also "needed" human worship in their temples.

In the chapter, we will discuss some of the biggest secrets of Ancient Egypt (some are related to some of these deities).

Chapter 6: Secrets of Ancient Egypt

You can probably say a lot of things about Ancient Egypt. You can characterize it as a country of riches, as a cradle of ancient civilization, and you can even blame them for being among the first to make use of slavery.

However you look at it, you can never say Egypt was boring, or simple, or in any way easy to understand (especially through the sensitivities and perspective of us, mere modern mortals).

The secrets of Ancient Egypt will always fascinate us, and they will keep on fueling our craziest stories and our most amazing corners of the imagination. Being a civilization so far away in time and a culture so fundamentally different than anything Western in so many ways, Egypt will never be an open book.

But that is exactly what makes it amazing. The secrets of Ancient Egypt might be found, one day. And we might be able to tell our grandchildren about the sometimes downright kooky explanations we have found for the mysteries of a place and time we simply did not understand enough.

Until then, we should all delight ourselves with these riddles. They are equally stimulating as they are revealing of our true nature as human beings: curious, restless, and thirsty for knowledge.

In this chapter, we will discuss some of the most powerful, intriguing, and interesting secrets of Ancient Egypt. We will cover all the essentials: from the things we cannot explain to the mysterious stories of Egypt and to the discoveries that have enriched our understanding of the ancient world.

Of course, you might be familiar with some of these stories and artifacts. Some of them have even been mentioned, at least briefly, in this book. But in this chapter, we will look at them through an entirely different lens: that of the questions they have still left unanswered for us.

I know this will be a fascinating topic for you, so I will not drag it on any longer. Let's dive right into the Ancient Egypt enigmas that still baffle us.

Ancient Egypt and Its Unexplained Secrets

Although significant advances have been made over the past century in determining many aspects of Egyptian culture and history, the truth is that many questions are still unanswered.

As always, questions left without an answer tend to lead to quite a lot of speculation—and sometimes, theories go as far as say that Egyptians had a bit of "outer space" to help build such a great civilization with means that were limited for the time.

I cannot claim to be able to list *all* the unexplained secrets of a civilization and culture that spanned over **three millennia** in just a fragment of a book. However, I will try to bring together the most baffling ones.

The Death of King Tut

King Tutankhamun is one of the single most famous pharaohs in Egypt—or so we see him, the modern people visiting his exhibits at the British Museum and listening to the stories (of horror, sometimes) that have been born out of this discovery.

In reality, as it has already been mentioned earlier in the book, King Tut was neither famous during his own life, nor did he live an exceptionally accomplished life. It would have been hard since he was a child when he became the king of Egypt and merely a very young man when he passed away.

Just as his tomb is surrounded by mystery, his death is too quite the riddle as well. It is clear that King Tut was very young when he passed away, so old age and the diseases usually associated with it are out of the discussion.

Even more, the fact that the mummification process seemed to have taken a different path in the case of King Tut suggests that his body was "fixed" after some sort of severe trauma.

As also mentioned before, his tomb seems to be very small compared to those of other pharaohs also suggests his death came completely by surprise (so his family had to improvise).

One of the most widespread theories related to King Tutankhamon's death suggests that he died by a hippo as he was trying to hunt it. Other theories say that he died in a chariot accident.

And finally, other theories say that King Tut was the result of incest (as his mother and father were also brother and sister), and as such, his body was weakened and imperfect. For instance, it is believed that he had clubbed foot, which means he couldn't have stood up on his own, which automatically excludes the chariot or hunting accident out of the picture (The Jerusalem Post, 2014).

The Burial Ground of Alexander the Great

Given that Alexander the Great was, you know, one of the guys who came *really* close to ruling the entirety of the (known) Earth, it is quite the mystery why people still can't figure out where he's buried.

Alexander the Great was not Egyptian. He was, as you probably know, Macedonian. However, he did conquer Egypt. Even more, he didn't do it just like that: he was mostly seen as a liberator, which is also why Egyptians declared him the son of god Amun.

The life of Alexander the Great is not *that* much of a mystery—but his death sure is. Although it seems that he asked to be thrown in the Euphrates River, it seems that his followers did not quite listen to his last wish. He was buried in Memphis, then moved to Alexandria, and then his body completely disappeared.

There are more than 140 recorded searches for Alexander the Great's tomb, but nobody has ever been able to identify where his remains lie. Maybe, as he had initially wanted, he was actually taken away by his father, god Amun (Bianchi, 2004).

Queen Nefertiti

Most people know at least two female names to come from Ancient Egypt's royalty: Cleopatra and Nefertiti.

While the first (who, historically, was the *last*) is quite well-known, and there is plenty of archeological and historical data to follow through her footsteps in life, the latter is not as transparent.

You see, Nefertiti did exist. There is no doubt about that. She ruled alongside her husband, Pharaoh Akhenaten. But then, after his death, it seems that she just vanished into thin air. We don't have any records of what happened to her afterwards, and it is still uncertain if her mummy has been discovered or not.

Some theorize that, during his life, Nefertiti became Akhenaten's co-regent (History.com, 2019),so after his death, she changed her name to Neferneferuaten and kept on ruling over Egypt. Other theories say that she took the name of Smenkhkare and ruled Egypt disguised as a man. No matter how you look at this, it seems rather mysterious that a Queen of Egypt would just disappear after her husband's death — so neither theories are downright crazy. Hopefully, time will tell, and we will be able to determine where her mummy is hidden, as well as whether or not she continued to rule over the kingdom of Egypt after Akhenaten's death.

The Great Pyramid of Giza

There are SO many mysteries surrounding the Great Pyramid that one could easily write an entire book just on that.

For starters, it is the largest and most flawless pyramid in all of Egypt. As explained earlier in the book, not all pyramids were pointy, and they were definitely not as tall and imposing as Khufu's pyramid.

That's pretty much where all our knowledge of this pyramid stops, though. How did Egyptians manage to create something so geometrically perfect, and how exactly did they even manage to *carry* all the blocks needed to build it? A deep-seated mystery covered in sand, time, and secret.

Even more than that, it seems that the Great Pyramid has *a lot* of chambers we do not fully understand the purpose of. Archeologists thought they had a pretty good idea of how many chambers there were in the pyramid, but just when they were about to confirm what they believed to be a near-certainty that two more chambers and several very thin tunnels were discovered. And if there are these chambers we did not know of, how many are there *really*? And why are they all so hidden and so mysterious? (Boult, 2016).

The Nabta Playa Stone Circle

If you thought the Stonehenge is mysterious, wait until you hear about the Nabta Playa Stone Circle. Discovered in the 1970s, this collection of dubiously well-arranged rocks seems eerily similar to those at Stonehenge.

Most theories point to the idea that the Nabta Playa were built for the same purpose (something related to astrology or perhaps some sort of religion or god we're not familiar with just yet). However, since the Nabta Playa Stone Circle is not yet fully uncovered (and it's more reconstructed than just *discovered* as such), it is likely that we will not find the answer to this mystery very soon.

The Sphinx and...the Second Sphinx

Everyone knows the Sphinx—the big guy guarding over the Pyramids of Giza. Although the purpose of his construction is not yet fully clear, what is perhaps even more baffling is that he's not alone.

No, I'm not talking about aliens, but the Second Sphinx was discovered in Israel in 2013. As it seems, Israeli archeologists stumbled upon the feet of what seems to be a smaller version of the Sphinx we all know (and love).

However, this structure is surrounded by a lot of mystery. To begin with, nobody has any clue how the Sphinx got there in the first place. While it seems that it was connected to King Mycerinus and that it was built more than 4,000 years ago, not much else is known.

Not to mention that archeologists don't have any idea of where the remainder of the Sphinx could be located!

They have plans to excavate the entire region, but the sad news about all that is that they have to search through a LOT of sand. More specifically, 600 years' worth of sand excavations, so we are not predicted to find the answers to our "Second Sphinx" questions very soon (CNN, 2013).

The Sphinx's Nose

Speaking of the Sphinx, if you look at a picture closely, you will probably notice somethingthere's something missing from the "face" of the Sphinx.

Apparently, its nose hasn't been where it should be for a very long time, but it is still not known how this happened, why, or even when exactly.

For a long while there, people believed that Napoleon's crews more or less accidentally shot the Sphinx's nose (which sounds ridiculous, I know). However, drawings of the Sphinx that date long before Napoleon show the giant structure as "nose-less" as it is today,so that theory is definitely not correct.

Another theory (which hasn't been proven or disproven yet) says that a Sufi Muslim king destroyed the Sphinx's nose when peasants prayed to it for rain and a successful harvest. Although there is no real proof this theory is the real one, it has at least not been disproven yet (Smithsonian Journeys, 2020)

Discoveries Made in Egypt

There are hundreds, if not thousands, of large and small discoveries made in Egypt. Just earlier this year, in 2020, Egyptian archeologists uncovered 59 sealed sarcophagi, for example (Nugali, 2020).

Obviously, there is a lot we still do not know or understand about Ancient Egypt. And frankly, the chances are that these things will remain a mystery for a long, long time from now on as well.

Every little discovery made in Egypt brings us closer to the past of a civilization that shaped the world (and our imagination too). As such, each discovery is very important in its own way. However, in this section of Chapter 6, I will walk you through some of the top most-interesting findings made in Egypt—the ones that elicit our thinking and bring us a little closer to understanding Egyptians (or, at times, raising new and important questions about them).

The following discoveries have given egyptologists (and the world) a treasure trove of understanding when it comes to Ancient Egyptian culture and civilization. At the same time, though, some of them have raised some pretty heavy questions as well.

Let's take a closer look at them!

The Valley of the Golden Mummies

In 1994, Dr. Zahi Hawass and his team made a great discovery at the Bahariya Oasis. About 211 miles away from the Great Pyramids, they found a two-square mile necropolis containing *a lot* of tombs. Upon excavating four of them, they also discovered no less than 105 mummies in there, many of which were wearing beautiful golden masks. This is how the name of this discovery was born.

Archeologists determined that this cemetery had been built during Roman Egypt. Although there were no inscriptions (which made it difficult for them to identify the mummies), this place gave Egyptologists a better understanding of this particular time of Egypt.

In their excavations, they also found four types of mummies:

- Gilded
- Covered in cartonnage
- In anthropoid coffins
- Wrapped in linen

It is believed that the gilded mummies pertained to the richest inhabitants of these tombs (they were most likely well-off merchants, for example). Even more, archeologists assume that entire families are buried here, as in some instances archeologists uncovered mothers, fathers, and children buried together.

The Valley of the Golden Mummies was discovered entirely by accident when a donkey's leg fell through a hole. Upon trying to get the animal's leg out, the guard who had been chasing him noticed glittering in the distance—and so he knew that there must be something to uncover there. It is odd and saddening to think that, if a poor donkey had not been running away that day, it would have been a long time before the Golden Mummies were discovered (Ancient-Origins, 2014).

King Tut's Tomb

We have spoken extensively about King Tutankhamen's tomb, mostly because it is by far one of the most famous ones ever discovered. Leaving aside the mystery of how the tomb was almost intact and how exactly Tut died, there is still a lot this tomb has shown us.

As mentioned previously, King Tut was not an especially important pharaoh, as he only ruled for about one decade (and he was a mere child when the throne was left to him). His tomb, however, made him more famous in death than he was probably in life.

The riches and the artifacts discovered in King Tut's tomb also helped Egyptologists better understand Ancient Egyptians. Tutankhamen was buried in three coffins, and the last one (the one in which he lied) was made entirely out of gold. A black liquid had been poured all over the coffin.

Aside from the mummy, this discovery is important because the tomb had not been looted. That meant archeologists finally had a chance to see what a burial space looked like for Ancient Egyptians. They discovered more than one hundred artifacts in King Tut's tomb, and that was absolutely priceless for their understanding of the era (Mascort, n..d)

The Oxyrhynchus Papyri

At first sight, there is almost nothing fantastic or exciting about the Oxyrhynchus Papyri. They are exactly what their name suggests: a series of papyri discovered at Oxyrhynchus, a city that had been prosperous during the Greek rule over the Egyptians, but of which nothing remains today.

What is fascinating about these papyri is that they are quite intact. Most times, only scribbles on stones survived from the

Egyptians, but this specific set of papyri was actually in a good state for its vast majority.

Even more, the papyri revealed daily activities and common things Egyptians did back then. Among the papyri, archeologists also found a few copies of the New Testament, a clear indication that Christianity was already sweeping across the Mediterranean. The papyri date from 113 BCE to the fourth century, so this makes sense).

Indeed, there is nothing spectacular about this discovery—but it is one of the smaller things that helped historians understand the period leading to the end of the Empire a lot better (The National Library of Wales).

The Pyramid-Age Papyri

As mentioned above, not many papyri have survived to our age. Unlike stone writings, papyri tend to degrade considerably over time, so to have a papyrus that dates back to the Egyptian pyramid age is quite remarkable.

The oldest papyri in the world date back to the Old Kingdom, and they are more than 4,6000 years old. Although they have not been preserved in pristine condition, they have given us important clues about a long list of questions we were having about Ancient Egypt.

For example, this set of papyri taught us about Egyptian shipping, economy, and agriculture. It also showed us, with a bit more clarity, how the Great Pyramids were built. Although we might not have all the details, these papyri are a priceless treasure that has shed a lot of light on some of Ancient Egypt's mysteries (Stille, 2015).

Khoy's Cemetery

This is one of the latest discoveries made in Ancient Egypt—and one of the most unique ones too. The reason this place is so special is that its structure is L-shaped, and some parts of it were meant to mimic the appearance of the pyramids of the Fifth Dynasty.

The tombs are believed to belong to Khoy, a noble of the Old Kingdom who lived during the Fifth Dynasty. What is very interesting, however, is that it seems that this type of structure was used for individuals rather than kings.

This discovery is still being analyzed (since it was only made in 2019), but it is bound to reveal at least a few secrets from Ancient Egypt. We are very curious to see what they will uncover! (Essam, 2019).

The Mysterious Ancient Civilization of Egypt

There are many things we still grasp to understand the Ancient Civilization of Egypt. How they came to be and how it is that they ended up vanishing almost entirely over a few centuries, how is it that death was such a major player in their lives, and how did they manage to understand technology that was way beyond their time?

Many questions are still pending for answers, and it is likely that we will never understand *everything*. We do understand a lot more than we did, and this part of Chapter 6 is meant to prove exactly that.

In this last section, I wanted to walk you through some of the most unique, fascinating, and intriguing issues related to Ancient Egypt—to crown the entire book in a tone that shows just how many secrets Egyptians hid (and just how few of them are.

The Embalming Secrets of Ancient Egyptians

For a long time, we didn't quite understand how it is that Egyptians managed to embalm the bodies so well (especially since many of the mummies discovered were in a very good state).

It was only recently that archeologists stumbled upon a mummification workshop, and a lot of their questions were elucidated. This was when Egyptologists learned that mummification was not only not just for pharaohs, but that embalmers had different "packages" for different budgets and needs.

More attention was put into the mummification and embalming process of the rich, who were ready to pay more for the service, and less attention into the embalming of the not-so-rich. Much like a modern funerary house, these embalmers sold their services based on clear fees and very clear "target audiences."

Death was a business—and a profitable one since it was intrinsically linked to Egyptians' belief in the afterlife. Everybody needed embalming, and that's not only because families wanted to make sure their beloved ones will have a happy afterlife, but also because *they* were pretty afraid the dead would come back as ghosts.

The discovery of this workshop also helped archeologists have a clearer idea of how exactly the mummification process was developed and what it involved. With the help of chemists, they were able to determine almost all the "ingredients" used in the embalming process, which led to a whole new era in our understanding of Egyptians.

All in all, the embalming secrets of Ancient Egyptians continue to linger between myth, belief, and business. But new discoveries such as the one mentioned above make it a lot easier for us to add a scientific basis to all of it.

Why They Used Astronomy to Build the Great Pyramids

One of the main reasons pyramids (and specifically, the Great Pyramids of Giza) were so mysterious is related to the precision with which they were built.

As it turns out, we were looking at them through a much too modern sense, ruling out what might have been the main trigger behind all this precision: astronomy.

Like many other ancient civilizations, Egyptians treasured their astronomy dearly, and it took proper science to help them in everyday life. The Great Pyramids were built with so much geometrical precision that for a long time, we could just not understand how come a civilization that did not have the technological means to calculate matters this exactly managed to pull it off.

Apparently (and to many people's disappointment), it was not aliens that drove the building of the pyramids, but astronomy itself. Guiding themselves after the stars, Egyptians managed to create structures that point directly to the stars and the cardinal directions. Because the Universe is perfectly aligned, the pyramids nailed the kind of perfection we simply over-complicated in time.

Astronomy was a catalyst *and* a method for Egyptians, and we cannot but bow at their creativity and resourcefulness when it comes to these things. Sure, it might sound less exciting than ancient civilizations being visited by aliens. But even so, all this points to the fact that we might be, perhaps, a little too arrogant about our own evolution as a civilization. We only see everything through our own perspective but fail to understand that the ancients had an entirely different view of the world (and that it is not necessarily a view less advanced or less efficient than ours) (Brown, 2018).

The Book of the Dead

As I have mentioned again and again in this book, death was an essential element of every Egyptian's life. Rich or not, each Egyptian was headed "West," one way or another. And they all had to go through the same process to ensure that whatever happens to them in the afterlife is not going to be too hard on them.

The Book of the Dead is how we, mere modern mortals, have gotten to a point where we have a much better understanding of death rituals in Ancient Egypt. It is believed the Book of the Dead originated sometime in the Third Dynasty and that having such a book in your tomb was like knowing the answers to your exam beforehand—a way to "trick" your way into the good afterlife.

Furthermore, you might also find it interesting to know that The Book of the Dead was most likely never canonized, as no two copies that were ever found look the same. This means that pretty much every priest had their own version of it (and, just like mortuary dolls, these books became a fully-fledged business due to their afterlife value).

Some parts of the book tell us in detail about the process of dying and reaching the afterlife we might not have thought would be possible to have so far away in time. For example, the Book of the Dead explains how, after death, the body is taken to the Hall of Truth by Anubis, where they have to testify to 42 sins they have never actually committed. Once the testimony is over, the gods (Osiris, Anubis, and Thoth) and the 42 Judges retreat to confer and give the final verdict for the soul.

The Book of the Dead is both one of the biggest mysteries of Ancient Egypt and one of its most poignant revelations for us. In many ways, it is like a "bible" of Ancient Egyptians, and it has helped us grasp a lot of what was going on back then. Although not standardized and a collection of spells, rather than stories, this book can be easily considered to lie at the top of our cultural findings of Ancient Egypt (Mark, 2016).

Chapter 7: The End of the Empire

About a thousand years ago, an unknown author was writing about the fall of the Viking culture under the smooth "invasion" of Christianity. The story was called "Beowulf," and although it is a story about dragons and heroes, what it truly reflected was the end of a civilization.

In reality, nobody can mark the end of an era with absolute certainty. Viking culture ended in many ways before they were Christianized, and Egyptians ended in many ways before they lost it altogether. The same rule applies to cultural and historical eras that span over more than just one country, actually. For instance, there are several schools of thought with different opinions on when exactly the Dark Ages ended.

Likewise, it is not exactly certain when the Egyptian Empire ended. Like most empires, it started as a slow decay—and it ended in the annihilation of everything Ancient Egypt meant in terms of culture and civilization.

This chapter will explore how Ancient Egypt found its demise—and how its gods were put to rest.

The Beginning of the End

Empires do not rise overnight. And they most definitely don't fall overnight either.

Such was the case of the Egyptian Empire too. Signs of trouble to shape up on the horizon of the Nile River civilization starting with the height of its ascension, during the ruling of Ramses II.

On the one hand, the Egyptians were being attacked by Hittites (coming from modern-day Turkey) and lacked the technological means to create weapons that could compete with theirs. While the Egyptians had vast resources of bronze, they couldn't fight against the new, stronger metal the Hittites were bringing along iron.

On the other hand, the structural integrity of the Egyptian Empire was starting to crumble. Rebel kings like Amenmesse, the murder of Ramses III, and civil war all left their mark on the twelfth century BCE Egypt slowly cracking the unity of the Empire.

By the eleventh century, Egypt was already split in two. In the following centuries, the country would reunite and live short bursts glimmering in the shadow of the old Empire. Egypt's fate was broken, though, for all the little bursts of success it had from the eleventh to the seventh century BCE were short-lived. Eventually, the country split again, and again, and again, until it became easy prey for the surrounding civilizations.

Assyrians conquered Egypt in the seventh century BCE. Upheaval made them retire quite early and brought back Egypt to the Egyptians for about 140 years. But again, this was short-lived, too (especially when looking at the grand scheme of things).

Although the peace lasted for more than a century this time, Egypt was already a weakened country, relying mostly on Greek mercenaries for their army (as opposed to native Egyptians, like in the days of the previous dynasties).

In 525 BCE, Egypt was conquered by Persians. Less than two hundred years later, it was conquered by Alexander the Great.

And so began the end of the Empire as we know it. Heavily influenced by the Greek culture but still clinging to their Egyptian roots, the people on the banks of the Nile saw the demise of their historical glory. Over the course of the next three hundred years, Egypt survived under the Ptolemy (Greek) dynasty, but this was about to be its last sparkle (Dodson, 2011).

Cleopatra - The Last of the Legends

Cleopatra is one of the single most famous characters of all Ancient Egypt. Shakespeare wrote about her. Movies were made about her, and many speculations and scandals surrounded her life and personality too.

As I was mentioning earlier in the book, Cleopatra was not, in fact, actually Egyptian. She was of Greek descent, part of the Ptolemy Dynasty Alexander the Great brought to Egypt. Yet, she is frequently dubbed as the last of the great legends of the Ancient Empire.

The entire dynasty of the Ptolemy descendants supported local culture from every perspective. Temples were built. The religion was kept the same. And from many points of view, Egypt continued to exist in its more or less former shape, at least on the outside.

Inside, however, nothing was ever the same. Egypt was dying its last breaths.

Cleopatra was, no doubt, an agile leader and a very smart Queen. She ruled Egypt with cunning and intelligence and fought for what belonged to Egyptians. Unfortunately, much of her life is surrounded by mystery because there are no actual contemporary accounts of how she came to be, who she was, or what she actually did.

Born in 69 BCE, Cleopatra was the last Queen of Egypt. Her ploy to conquer Caesar's heart worked out as planned, but she ended up in a sea of intrigues that reflected upon Egypt's status. Her death, covered in as much mystery as her life, mirrored the end of the Empire as we know it.

In 30 BCE, Romans took charge of Egypt. (Dodson, 2011; History.com, 2019).

Egyptian Gods, Exist Scene to the West

Egypt was under Roman rule for more than 600 years. During this time, the trends, religions, and legislation of the Roman Empire and its ups and downs swept through the Nile civilization, changing its face entirely.

By the fourth century, Egypt's old ways were mostly focused on pockets of geographical areas. The hieroglyphic writing was slowly dying out under the influence of Greek Christian writings, and the Old gods had long retired, leaving room for Christianity.

In 640, the Arab invasion brought with it Islam, and Egypt changed once again. All that remains are the artifacts of a 3,000-year civilization that ruled over the Mediterranean and continues to fuel our imagination in the wildest, most amazing ways.

No doubt, current Egyptian culture is amazing in its own ways. Few ancient things (like the remains of Isis being worshiped) survive to the date, though.

Every empire rises, and every empire falls. It is a rule history has mercilessly imposed over everyone: Egyptians, Greeks, Romans, Assyrians, Aztecs, and many others. Gods enter the scene, and, at some point, their immortality dies out with the civilizations that brought them to the peak of their success.

What's left behind are priceless lessons, art, stories, and beauty, as well as sorrow and pain for the souls lost in the battles fought for the glory of a virtually invisible border.

Do we have a lot to learn from the Ancient Egyptians?

Most definitely.

Conclusion

Some 3,000 years ago, a culture on the banks of the Nile River was erecting what would, later on, be considered to be a wonder of the Ancient World. Little did they know that three millennia later, people would be paying tickets to go and see what were essentially their tombs.

Little did they know that their stories would make it to the Big Screens of Hollywood or that the stories of a king that only ruled for under a decade would fuel horror scenarios into the minds and culture of modern people.

And little did they know that in less than 3,000 years, their civilization was about to unfold itself at the feet of Rome under the shape of a gorgeous Queen of Greek descent.

Fate has its ways, though. And as I said earlier in the book, everything that rises must fall at one point or another too.

Egypt made no exception from this universal rule.

A Kingdom of sunlight and prosperity is never born out of thin air. It is born out of faith (and not necessarily faith in the gods, but faith in the power of humans). It is born out of devotement, passion, and love for growth.

Ancient Egypt was born on the banks of the Nile as a polytheistic society and died as a monotheistic one, showing that just a few hundred years can change mentalities and shift the culture of a people to 180.

Indeed, the Egypt of Ramses II was already going on a slippery slope by the time his rulership ended. But what is admirable is that it took many hundreds of years before his culture finally shifted into one of Christianity, and then of Islam. Egyptians stuck with their civilization and fought for it until the very end—and even today, marks of the civilization the first Kings built on the banks of the Nile keep on fueling dreams, intrigues, and "modern myths."

From cursed pharaoh tombs to aliens who were hand in hand with the Ancient Egyptians, the mystery of the Nile civilization has given birth to plenty of modern stories. Some of them are downright ludicrous; others are already decade-old and true legends in their own right.

It is easy to see why. We are looking, after all, at a culture and religion that happened more than 5,000 years ago, so it's clear that some misunderstanding and "make-belief" will make way into our understanding of these people.

There is yet much to uncover from the sand of Egypt; that's true. But that makes it even easier to see why there's an ongoing fascination with this land of promise, myth, and magic.

It is also easy to see why a culture basking in golden sands and golden tombs would be the target of thieves and the target of many misinterpretations.

With all our knowledge, it is hard for us to understand Ancient Egyptians. There is something equally morbid AND magic about their entire culture. It seems that they mostly lived to die (a concept certified by the attention with which they built their tombs). But at the same time, they do not seem to be people who did not know how to live (again, they actually did have a fascination with beer—so much so that they even included it in their origin myths).

We are, in so many ways, entirely different than our brethren Ancient Egyptians were. It's not just our religion that makes us different, though. It is how we see distances and time, the way we understand science today, and how each of us lives our lives in small ways and big ways alike.

And, at the end of the day, we are also incredibly similar. Egyptians were a culture distanced in time, space, and knowledge from us. But at their very core, they had the very same big questions as we do:

- How did life happen?
- Is there anything bigger that rules us?
- Where are we heading once all this is over?
- How to live better lives?
- How to make more money and buy more things?

- What do we ACTUALLY live behind?

Same as Greeks, Romans, Assyro-Babylonians, and Aztecs. Egyptians asked the big questions and gave their own version of an answer. Even with today's knowledge and technology, none of us can actually know for certain what the real answers to these questions are.

And just like Ancient Egyptians, we may choose to believe in one explanation or another.

We still erect big buildings, we still pray, and we still live our lives to leave a better world for our children. We still have heroes and villains, politics and wars, famine, and great natural disasters.

We still fight against diseases that plague our society, health, and economy.

From afar, Ancient Egyptians are as close to us as the fantasy characters of *Game of Thrones* are. They are incestuous, rabid for power, and they frequently fall in love with the wrong guys and girls.

Up close, they are just as human as we are—and that is both endearing and frightening to know. If nothing has really changed, in essence, in more than 5,000 years, how are we to say that our own civilization will not end in sadness and bitterness, just like that of the Ancient Egyptians?

Who will conquer us now?

Who will win?

And how will the next hundred years look like?

Will we ever find an answer to all those ardent questions?

Looking at our past should not be just a pastime that fuels our creativity and storytelling capabilities. It should be a lesson for the future. It should be the cautionary tale we all have to understand to avoid making the same mistakes.

Indeed, there is still a lot we can uncover from what Egyptians left behind. But even with our otherwise limited knowledge of these people, there are still important lessons to be drawn.

Like, for example, how balance can affect our entire view on life. If more of us strive for balance, as opposed to money or fame, the world would most definitely be a better place. The chances are that not even all of the Egyptian rules followed these lessons, and most times, it brought them an early end and a legacy worthy of villainous gods.

Another lesson is that you cannot change who people are just because you want them to be a certain way—or at least not instantaneously. Akhenaten tried and failed, and what is left behind from him are ruins and a genuinely unsuccessful attempt.

Every rulership, every pyramid, every tomb, and every small statue can all teach us important lessons not only about Egyptians themselves but about who we are, down inside. The things that really drive us, the fears that make us make rash decisions, the passions that fuel us to move forward, the internal wars we fight against chaos and disorder—they are all there, within us.

If you have followed this book closely, you have already learned that all these things are deeply buried under the sands of Egyptian culture and mythology as well.

The main goal of this book was not to reveal to you major truths about the future but to fuel your own curiosity in learning more about the cultures and civilizations that defined the past of our planet.

I hope I managed to achieve that. A lot more could be said about Egyptians and the world they left behind, but unfortunately, it would really take entire libraries to do it (as I have already emphasized throughout the book). Some of the things are small curiosities that paint more accurate pictures of Ancient Egypt (like, for example, the fact that most of the Kings were actually overweight). Others are major myths and stories that defined the rise and fall of entire dynasties. And others are mere suppositions people have made throughout time.

In between myth and historical fact, the civilization that rose and fell on the banks of the Nile River is a fascinating one from every standpoint. You don't have to be an avid fan of mythology to understand that Egyptians had a very interesting view of the Universe. And you do not have to be passionate about history to understand that 3,0000 years of Ancient Egyptian history are an intricate topic to discuss any way you put it.

I started with the great periods of the Egyptian Empire and how they defined the basic tenets of the cultures they ruled over. I ended with the final decades of the Egyptian Empire as painted through one of the last great acts of an Egyptian leader: conquering the heart of the greatest ruler in the world at that time to save her own kingdom.

In between, we have walked the fascinating path of the gods that mirrored Egypt, its fears, and its hopes. The god Ra, the ultimate life creator, the god of order, the god of chaos, the army of goddesses that were both peaceful and fierce—they all define how Egyptians actually saw other people, the nature surrounding them, and the historical events that affected their day to day lives.

That is the beauty of myths, in the end. They transpire through history, society, religion, and spirituality to create an image far deeper and more meaningful than any of those would do separately. Yes, they might not be scientifically accurate. And yes, your own religious beliefs might contradict them, but if there is one thing we have to really "give to" the ancients, they really did know how to create beautiful stories (and stories of fear and bloodshed too).

Myths have the amazing power to move the soul and fuel the mind in ways nothing else could ever do it. They help us get closer to our real nature, and ultimately, they help us understand life and death beyond mere facts.

From the beginning of mankind, as we know it, myths have been part of who we were. And although in a veiled shape, myths continue to shape our lives. Just look at how many people take over the cinema when a new Marvel or DC comics movie comes out. That is a clear sign that people, no matter their religion, still need to look up to something. They still need to believe that the fight between good and evil will always end with the first one winning and the latter losing.

Ancient Egyptians were no different. They made up stories that reflected their passions, fears, and the things they could not explain otherwise. But they also made up stories because they needed **hope**.

For them, death was not the end but the beginning of a new form.

The sun would always rise in the sky because there was a god who made sure this happened.

And balance would always win because, in the fight between Horus and Seth, the former won.

As the gods of Egypt passed into oblivion, these beliefs themselves took new forms, in new stories, and a new religion. Century after century, the culture of the Ancients reshaped to mirror the new realities.

Until, one day, there was nothing left of Ra, Horus, Isis, or Seth, but big buildings, artifacts, and stories inscribed on walls and papyri.

As a final food for thought, I challenge you to imagine life on Earth 3,000 years from now. What will be left of us and our beliefs? How will the people of the future know why, for example, we built bridges, trade centers, churches, mosques, and temples?

How will they interpret our wars? The fights for power?

How will they see our own fascination with the worlds gone by?

Will they understand our fears, motivators, and passions?

Will they understand how peace mattered more than anything to us, despite all the wars we fight?

Time will tell. But if we are to hope for something about how our own civilization will reflect on the next millennia, we can only hope we will be as fascinating for our successors as Egyptians have been for us. And ultimately, we can, maybe, hope that we will leave behind valuable lessons too.

Let both our understanding of our past and our next steps guide us towards that ideal scenario where we are seen as forefathers of a new world. Let our empathy and compassion rule supreme and leave behind a world shinier, brighter, and more fascinating than anything that came before us!

It is in our power to create that future.

Let's do it!

Subscribe To Sofia Visconti

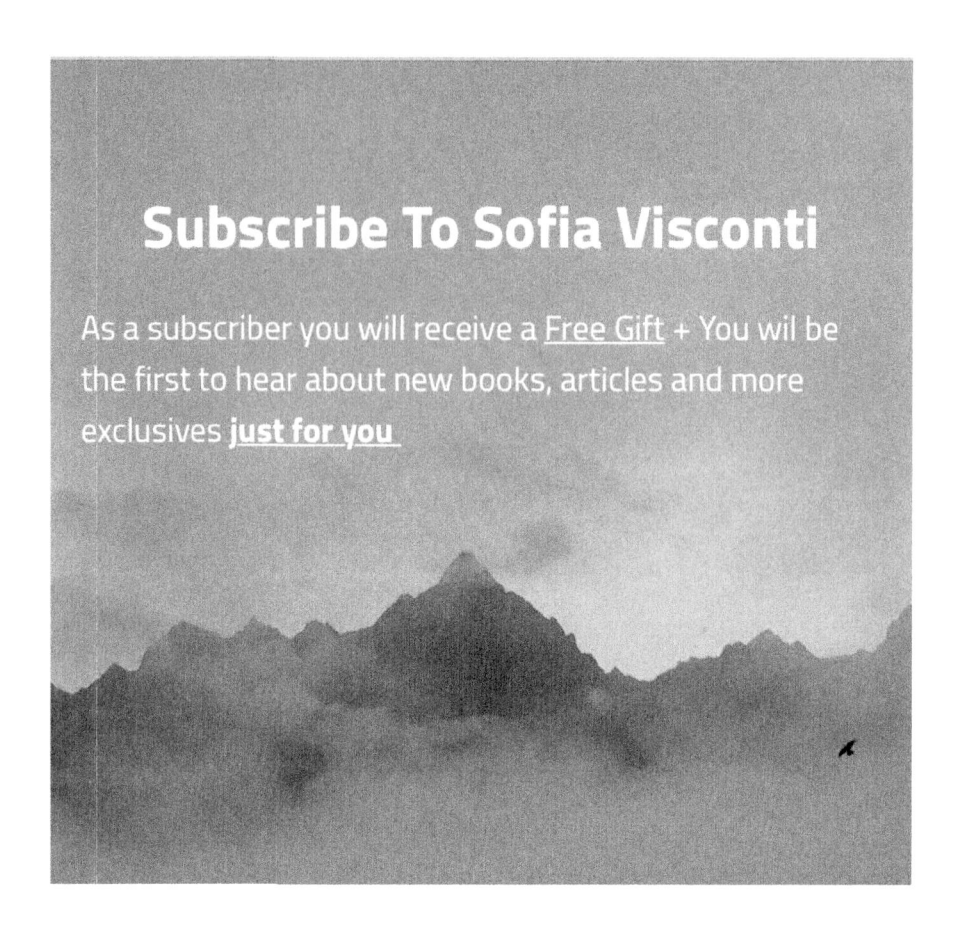

As a subscriber you will receive a Free Gift + You wil be the first to hear about new books, articles and more exclusives *just for you*

Click Here

References

Ancient Egypt Online. *The Ancient Egyptian Calendar.* https://www.ancient-egypt-online.com/ancient-egyptian-calendar.html

Ancient Origins. (2014). *The Valley of the Golden Mummies and a wealth of knowledge about our ancient past.* Ancient-origins.net. https://www.ancient-origins.net/ancient-places-africa/valley-golden-mummies-and-wealth-knowledge-about-our-ancient-past-002172

Andrews, E. (2020, Jan 30). *11 Things You May Not Know About Ancient Egypt.* HISTORY. https://www.history.com/news/11-things-you-may-not-know-about-ancient-egypt

Bellis, M. (2019). *The Invention of the Wheel.* ThoughtCo. https://www.thoughtco.com/the-invention-of-the-wheel-1992669

Bianchi, R. (2004, November 11). The Elusive Tomb of Alexander. Archaeology Magazine Archive. https://archive.archaeology.org/online/features/alexander/tomb.html

Boult, A. (2016). *Scientists discover two mysterious 'chambers' in the Great Pyramid of Giza.* The Telegraph. https://www.telegraph.co.uk/science/2016/10/18/scientists-discover-two-mysterious-chambers-in-the-great-pyramid/

Brier, B. (2001). *The History of Ancient Egypt.* Teaching Co.

Brogan, J. (2017, October 11). *Why the Ancient Egyptians Loved Their Kitties.* Smithsonian Magazine. https://www.smithsonianmag.com/smithsonian-institution/why-ancient-egyptians-loved-their-kitties-180965155/

Brown, D. (2018, March 14). Astronomy can help us unlock the secrets of the Egyptian pyramids. The Independent. https://www.independent.co.uk/news/science/pyramids-how-build-egypt-astronomy-giza-stonehenge-ancient-people-a8252211.html

Brunner, H. (n.d.). *Hieroglyphic Writing*. Encyclopedia Britannica. https://www.britannica.com/topic/hieroglyphic-writing

Bunson, M. (2002). *Encyclopedia of Ancient Egypt*.

Campbell, J. (2008). *The Hero with a Thousand Faces*. New World Library.

CNN. (2013, August 9). *Mystery surrounds Egyptian sphinx unearthed in Israel*. CNN. https://edition.cnn.com/2013/08/08/world/meast/israel-sphinx/index.html.

Discovering Egypt. (n.d.) *Ancient Egyptian Game of Senet*. https://discoveringegypt.com/ancient-egyptian-game-senet/

Dodson, A. (2011, February 17). BBC - History - Ancient History in depth: Egypt: The End of a Civilisation. Bbc.co.uk. http://www.bbc.co.uk/history/ancient/egyptians/egypt_end_01.shtml.

Oldest.org. (n.d.) 10 Oldest Mummies in the World. https://www.oldest.org/culture/mummies/

Egyptian Myths.. (n.d.). The Princess of Bekhten. http://www.egyptianmyths.net/mythbekhten.htm

Essam, A. (2019, April 13). *In pic: All what you need to know about the one of a kind Khuwy tomb*. EgyptToday.

https://www.egypttoday.com/Article/4/68261/In-pic-All-what-you-need-to-know-about-the

Fraser, K. (2014). *Before They Were Belly Dancers*. McFarland & Company.

Greshko, M. (2017, November 2). *Mysterious Void Discovered in Egypt's Great Pyramid*. https://www.nationalgeographic.com/news/2017/11/great-pyramid-giza-void-discovered-khufu-archaeology-science/

Grimal, N. (1992). *History of Ancient Egypt*. Blackwell Pr.

Haikal, F (n.d.). *Ra, The Creator God of Ancient Egypt*. Arce.org. https://www.arce.org/resource/ra-creator-god-ancient-egypt

Hansen, N. (2020, June 28). *11 Things You Didn't Know About Isis And Osiris*. The Collector. https://www.thecollector.com/isis-and-osiris/

Herodotus. (2017). *An Account of Egypt*. Sheba Blake Publishing

HISTORY. (2019, September 30). *Egyptian Pyramids.*. https://www.history.com/topics/ancient-history/the-egyptian-pyramids

HISTORY. (2019, June 8). *Nefertiti*. https://www.history.com/topics/ancient-history/nefertiti

Hoch, J. (n.d.). *Egyptian language*. Encyclopedia Britannica. https://www.britannica.com/topic/Egyptian-language

India Today. (2016, December 5). *6 famous mummies and the fascinating stories behind them*. https://www.indiatoday.in/education-today/gk-current-affairs/story/famous-mummies-355775-2016-12-05

Leveille, D. (2015, May 11). As Chile's climate changes, the world's oldest mummies are turning moldy. The World from PRX. https://www.pri.org/stories/2015-05-11/chiles-climate-changes-worlds-oldest-mummies-are-turning-moldy

Lichtheim, M. (2006). *Ancient Egyptian Literature*. University of California Press.

Marie, M. (2019, December 8). *DNA tests used to determine Nefertiti's mummy*. Egypt Today. https://www.egypttoday.com/Article/4/78496/DNA-tests-used-to-determine-Nefertiti%E2%80%99s-mummy

Mark, J. (2013, January 19). *Ancient Egyptian Burial*. Ancient History Encyclopedia. https://www.ancient.eu/Egyptian_Burial/

Mark, J. (2016, July 29). *Amun*. Ancient History Encyclopedia. https://www.ancient.eu/amun/

Mark, J. (2016, November 14). *Ancient Egyptian Literature*. Ancient History Encyclopedia. https://www.ancient.eu/Egyptian_Literature/

Mark, J. (2016, July 25). *Anubis*. Ancient History Encyclopedia. https://www.ancient.eu/Anubis/#

Mark, J. (2016, March 24). *Egyptian Book of the Dead*. Ancient History Encyclopedia. https://www.ancient.eu/Egyptian_Book_of_the_Dead/

Mark, J. (2016, March 24). *Egyptian Gods - The Complete List*. Ancient History Encyclopedia. https://www.ancient.eu/article/885/egyptian-gods---the-complete-list/

Mark, J. (2016, March 6). *Osiris*. Ancient History Encyclopedia. https://www.ancient.eu/osiris/.

Mark, J. (2016, March 18). *Pets in Ancient Egypt.* Ancient History Encyclopedia. https://www.ancient.eu/article/875/pets-in-ancient-egypt/#

Mark, J. (2016, March 7). *Set (Egyptian God).* Ancient History Encyclopedia. https://www.ancient.eu/Set_(Egyptian_God)/

Mark, J. (2016, July 26). *Thoth.* Ancient History Encyclopedia. https://www.ancient.eu/Thoth/

Mark, J. (2017, May 30). *A Brief History of Egyptian Art.* Ancient History Encyclopedia. https://www.ancient.eu/article/1077/a-brief-history-of-egyptian-art/

Mark, J. (2017, March 16). *Beer in Ancient Egypt.* Ancient History Encyclopedia. https://www.ancient.eu/article/1033/beer-in-ancient-egypt

Mascort, M (n.d.). *Close Call: How Howard Carter Almost Missed King Tut's Tomb.* National Geographic. https://www.nationalgeographic.com/history/magazine/2018/03-04/findingkingtutstomb/

Meehan, E (n.d.). *Anubis.* Mythopedia. https://mythopedia.com/egyptian-mythology/gods/anubis/

The Metropolitan Musuem of Art. (n.d.). List of Rulers of Ancient Egypt and Nubia. https://www.metmuseum.org/toah/hd/phar/hd_phar.htm

Moyers, B. (1988, June 22). *Ep. 2: Joseph Campbell and the Power of Myth — 'The Message of the Myth.'* Bill Moyers. https://billmoyers.com/content/ep-2-joseph-campbell-and-the-power-of-myth-the-message-of-the-myth/

Nugali, N. (2020, October 3). *Egyptian archaeologists unveil discovery of 59 sealed sarcophagi*. Arab News. https://www.arabnews.com/node/1743621/middle-east

Parra, J (n.d.). *Standing Tall: Egypt's Great Pyramids*. National Geographic. https://www.nationalgeographic.com/history/magazine/2017/01-02/egypt-great-pyramids-giza-plateau/

Pilkington, E. (2007, June 27). *Tooth solves Hatshepsut mummy mystery*. The Guardian. https://www.theguardian.com/world/2007/jun/27/egypt.science

Pruitt, S. (2019, May 9). *Ancient Egypt's 10 Most Jaw-Dropping Discoveries*. HISTORY. https://www.history.com/news/ancient-egypt-10-best-discoveries-king-tut-pyramids

Rawlinson, K. (2018, November 6). *New discovery throws light on mystery of pyramids' construction*. The Guardian. https://www.theguardian.com/world/2018/nov/06/new-discovery-throws-light-on-mystery-of-pyramids-construction

Roebuck, C. (1966). *The World of Ancient Times*. C. Scribner Sons.

San Jose State University (n.d.). *The Timeline of the Life of Cleopatra*. https://www.sjsu.edu/faculty/watkins/cleopatra.htm

Slackman, M. (2008, November 16). *In the Shadow of a Long Past, Patiently Awaiting the Future* (2008, November 16). The New York Times. https://www.nytimes.com/2008/11/17/world/middleeast/17cairo.html

Smithsonian (n.d). *The Egyptian Pyramid*. https://www.si.edu/spotlight/ancient-egypt/pyramid

Smithsonian Journeys. (2020, May 2020). *What happened to the Sphinx's nose?* https://www.smithsonianjourneys.org/blog/photo-what-happened-to-the-sphinxs-nose-180950757/

Spence, L. (1990). *Ancient Egyptian Myths and Legends* (1st ed.). General Publisher Company.

Stewart, J. (2018, November 22). *7 Surprising Facts About the Egyptian Pyramids.* My Modern Met. https://mymodernmet.com/egyptian-pyramids/#

Stille, A. (2015, October 25). *The World's Oldest Papyrus and What It Can Tell Us About the Great Pyramids.* Smithsonian Magazine. https://www.smithsonianmag.com/history/ancient-egypt-shipping-mining-farming-economy-pyramids-180956619/

The Jerusalem Post. (2014, October 26). *New evidence sheds light on King Tut's death.* https://www.jpost.com/Middle-East/King-Tut-was-the-product-of-an-incestuous-relationship-new-evidence-suggests-379862

The National Library of Wales (n.d). *The Oxyrhynchus Papyri.* https://www.library.wales/discover/digital-gallery/manuscripts/the-early-ages/the-oxyrhynchus-papyri

White, B. (2003, August 11). *Ancient Egypt Provides an Early Example of How A Society's Worldview Drives Engineering and the Development of Science.* http://www.strategic-tech.org/images/Egyptian_Engineering_and_Culture.pdf

Wilkins, R. (1992). *Neurosurgical Classics.* American Association of Neurological Surgeons.

Wolkoff, J. (2020, March 3). *How ancient Egyptian cosmetics influenced our beauty rituals.* CNN. https://edition.cnn.com/style/article/ancient-egypt-beauty-ritual-artsy/index.html

Worrall, S. (n.d.). *The Truth Behind Egypt's Female Pharoahs and Their Power.* https://www.nationalgeographic.com/culture/2018/12/queens-egypt-pharaohs-nefertiti-cleopatra-book-talk

Zorich, Z. (2016, March 29). *5 Unsolved Mysteries of King Tut's Tomb.* Scientific American. https://www.scientificamerican.com/article/5-unsolved-mysteries-of-king-tut-s-tomb/